TRIUMPHANT IN TROUBLE

TRIUMPHANT IN TROUBLE

STUDIES IN I PETER

by
PAUL S. REES

FLEMING H. REVELL COMPANY

To
EVANGELINE
Only Survivor, with Me, of Our
Parental Family
Where Both of Us Were Taught the Holy
Art of
"Resting in childlike trust upon His will
Who moves to His great ends unthwarted by the ill"

CONTENTS

I
AN EPISTLE UNDER THE MICROSCOPE

I

AN EPISTLE UNDER THE MICROSCOPE

Skip this chapter!

An absurd thing to say, especially if it were intended to apply to *all* readers. Why burden a book with a chapter that may be passed over without loss?

The reply is that, in the circumstances, any prospective reader is entitled to an option: either to read a summary of what the scholars say in analysis and appraisal of the *First Epistle of Peter*, or, forgoing this, to plunge straight into the letter itself. The latter course is neither foolish nor fruitless. It would be stupid only if one were to say or imply that textual and historical criticism is of no value.

What, now, do I mean by "in the circumstances"? This book, though full of comment, is not strictly a commentary. The material it contains was delivered in condensed form to a congregation of more than four thousand Christians in a succession of four days, a fact that will explain why the style, here and there, is informal. The *preacher* conquers the *author*.

In these addresses, moreover, the purpose that ruled was that of showing the *relevance* of what Peter wrote, both to the Christians for whom the writing was originally intended and to Christians now. For the achievement of such a purpose sheer exegesis is never enough.

One might add that for the accomplishment of such a purpose it is not acutely important to know whether or not, as one novel theory now has it,[1] *I Peter* is the clergyman's part in a formal baptismal service held on Easter Day. On the far horizon of

---

[1] The view of Professor F. L. Cross, set out in *I Peter: a Paschal Liturgy*, Mowbrays, London: 1954.

Peter's vision, and in the near places of his own heart, were these Christians who were always exposed to misrepresentation and insecurity and were, in the apostle's day, moving closer and closer to the sevenfold heat of the enemy's fiery furnace. They needed to be built and braced for the ordeal. To meet this need a literary vehicle was created which, in the compass of 105 verses, gives us what Dean Selwyn calls a "microcosm of Christian faith and duty, the model of a pastoral charge". That vehicle is *I Peter*.

The throb of this epistle's solicitous love and the thrust of its high summons will reach us whether we know a blessed thing about the technical jargon of the Petrine scholars: "Descensus ad Infernos", "Verba Christi", "Form Criticism", the "Subordinationist Principle", "Catechumen Forms", and all the rest.

The Christian *can* be "Triumphant in Trouble". Peter knows it. He wants his Christian friends in Asia Minor to know it—and to demonstrate it.

Hence for those who are, above all, concerned to suck the marrow out of the content of this epistle of courage and hope, it may be said, not facetiously, Skip this opening chapter and get on with the main business at hand!

On the other hand, there are readers whose curiosity includes a concern over such matters as the *historical context* of the epistle, its *format* and *style*, its *distinctive features*, and, not to be omitted, the *problems* it raises for the scholars.

I make no attempt at a formal discussion of these matters. The attempt, if made, would not ring true. I am not a scholar. It is perhaps not vain to think that I am a student, with a student's honest respect for authentic scholarship. The reverse side of this respect is a disinclination to be dazzled by the airy pretensions of some authorities who have difficulty drawing a distinction between a fanciful theory and a reasonable assumption of fact.

Let me simply indicate the position taken in this book, with due allowance for other viewpoints and with recognition that in some areas of research further and fuller light may yet break upon us.

A. DERIVATION

Both *authorship* and *literary sources* are here involved.

I believe that when the available data are weighed judiciously we are entitled to retain the traditional view that the Apostle Peter gave us this letter. It is to be suspected that Peter has had my "bias" all along. Still, so far as I am able to be objective, I believe "on points" Selwyn wins over Beare.[1] Says Professor Cranfield: "The statement of Beare that 'there can be no possible doubt that "Peter" is a pseudonym' is far more dogmatic than the present state of scholarly discussion warrants."[2] Beyond concurring in that judgment by this Durham University lecturer I should like to suggest that it is a delightful example of the British fondness for *understatement*.

To what extent has Peter, with the assistance of Silvanus, drawn on other New Testament writings? As one reads the letter he hears echoes of Romans, Ephesians, I and II Thessalonians, and James, to mention those where the parallels are perhaps most easily recognized. Does "coincidence" explain the resemblances? If not, what?

Did Peter borrow from Paul? Or did Paul borrow from Peter? Or did both draw from sources that circulated more or less freely among the churches of their day?

The third option has increasing support from competent scholars. It appears that *baptismal, catechetical* and *ethical-teaching* forms were in general use. Moreover, the *kerygma*, the proclaimed substance of the apostolic preaching, may be regarded as a verbal trust, which, well defined, bound the

---

[1] Cf. E. G. Selwyn, *The First Epistle of St. Peter* (Macmillan and Co., New York: 1946, 2nd ed.), pp. 7–115, and F. W. Beare, *The First Epistle of Peter* (Basil, Blackwell, and Mott, Oxford: 1945, Rev. 1958) pp. 1–41. Selwyn's support of the position that Silvanus was more than an amanuensis for Peter, that he was in all probability a collaborator, thus accounting for the excellence of the Greek in *I Peter*, may seem a bit strained, but the total impact of his argument is impressive.

[2] Cranfield, *I and II Peter and Jude*, SCM Press, p. 16.

churches together in a common witness before the world. This was in wide circulation, we may believe, before the New Testament documents were one by one produced under the direction of the Holy Spirit. The contributions of Dodd and Selwyn, acknowledged by such men as Barclay and Walls, bring this view well within the circle of credibility. The parallels between the *preaching* that we find in Acts and the interpretations of the Gospel found in *I Peter* are particularly close and striking.[1] It is easy, therefore, to understand how sayings of Jesus that were not recorded in the Four Gospels, together with formulas for baptismal services and for instruction of converts, were woven, sometimes consciously, sometimes unconsciously, into the text of the letters produced both by Paul and Peter.

B. DESTINATION

The Christians of five districts of Asia Minor are to be the recipients of this letter: Pontus, Galatia, Cappadocia, Asia, and Bithynia. Asia, of course, does not mean the continent. Walls holds that three separate parts of this large district were called by the provincial name. Galatia is taken by some to mean in this case North Galatia. With both of these possibilities in mind—that "Asia" means a northern area of the province and that "Galatia" means the northerly half of it—it is not unreasonable to believe that the Apostle Peter's scattered flock lay in that part of Asia Minor which the Apostle Paul did not evangelize.

In any case, they were a mixture of Jews and Gentiles, the latter probably in the majority. Who more than Gentile believers could appreciate the significance of Peter's reminder in chapter 2, verse 10: "Once you were no people, but now you are God's people"?

On the other hand, who more than converts from Judaism could grasp with ease the numerous allusions Peter makes to

[1] Cf. William Barclay, *The Letters of James and Peter* (St. Andrew Press, Edinburgh; The Westminster Press, Philadelphia: 1960), pp. 166–8.

Old Testament Scriptures and the decidedly "Levitical" picture of the Church that he introduces in chapter 2, verse 2.

Calvin may have insisted that the Churches addressed were made up of Jewish disciples, and Augustine may have argued that they were formed out of Gentile stock, but the total evidence would appear to call for a rejection of the dilemma in favour of a fellowship of believers drawn from both sources.

C. DATE

New Testament researchers have, in the main, favoured three periods within which the epistle may have been written: (1) in the reign of Trajan, or about A.D. 111; (2) the reign of Domitian, between A.D. 90 and 100; and (3) the reign of Nero, or about A.D. 62–64. Either of the late dates rules out the Petrine authorship. Since we have rested our case with the belief that this is a letter produced by none other than the apostle, we hold with Walls that "The most satisfactory date is a little before the outbreak of the Neronian persecution, in A.D. 63 or early 64".[1] J. B. Phillips is of the same mind. With most scholars who accept the Petrine authorship, he sees Rome (the "Babylon" of 5: 13) as the scene of the writing shortly before Nero lifted the floodgate of savagery against the Christians.

D. DISTINCTIVES

In Content

1. A conspicuous feature of the epistle is formed by the so-called "persecution passages": 1: 6–7; 3: 13–17; 4: 12–19; and 5: 9. It is chiefly in these that we learn of the troubled lot of the Christians in Asia Minor. The phrase in verse 6 of chapter

---

[1] A. F. Walls, in "Introduction" of *The First Epistle General of Peter*, in the Tyndale series of commentaries (Wm. B. Eerdmans Publishing Co., Grand Rapids: 1959; I.V.F.: London), page 67. I cannot too highly praise what he has achieved in this excellent introductory essay. A Lecturer in Theology at Fourah Bay College in Sierra Leone, he has given us, in slightly more than 50 pages, a discussion of the historical and critical data associated with *I Peter* that is a marvel of comprehensiveness and condensation.

1, "to suffer various trials", may be taken as symbolic of the large context of trouble within which the apostle sees these believers whom he is addressing. The Greek word for trials (*peirasmoi*), as Selwyn points out, covers "every kind of opposition and slander . . . whether coming from Jewish leaders, or from the leaders of Gentile religions such as the Asiarchs or Bithyniarchs, or from Roman authorities, or from society at large".[1]

However, neither in chapter 1 nor in chapter 2 is there anything to indicate that the sufferings encountered are due to public policy or are linked with a form of persecution in which it was considered a crime merely to bear the name of "Christian". The harassments and pains of 1: 6–7 and 3: 13–17 may be regarded as private in the sense that they could easily arise from the hostility of neighbours or the caprice of local officials rather than overt and widespread oppression by government.

The case is different, so it has been felt, in the passage that occurs in chapter 4. Beare, for example, gives it as his judgment that the paragraph beginning with verse 12 "breathes an entirely different atmosphere. . . . Suffering is no longer contemplated as a vague possibility for which Christians must always be prepared; it has become a stark actuality in the 'fiery ordeal' which is putting their faith to the test".[2]

In itself this observation is not one to evoke dissent. It must be pointed out, however, that Beare presses the radically different character of this allusion to persecution in the interest of his total theory concerning the epistle. He views this document as a second-century production by some unknown author who appropriated Peter's name and prestige. Accordingly, the persecution the writer has in mind is one in which, as under Trajan, "Christianity is in itself a crime deserving of death".[3]

---

[1] *Op. cit.*, p. 53. [2] *Op. cit.*, p. 7.
[3] *Ibid.*, p. 11. The quotation is taken by Beare from Professor W. M. Ramsay. Those desiring to pursue this critical problem further will find a wealth of material in the "Introduction" to *I Peter* of such scholars as Selwyn, Beare, Barclay, Walls, and Bigg.

It may be worthless as evidence, but I must say that I read *I Peter* for many years prior to Beare, Perdelwitz, Cross, and others without being aware that the "fiery ordeal" of 4: 12 *must* be taken as radically different from the being "tested by fire" of 1: 7. Is it not possible that Beare, and those of his persuasion regarding a late date for this letter, have exaggerated the significance of certain details, such as, for example, the writer's use of the phrase "reproached for the name of Christ" in 4: 14? After all, our Lord predicted sufferings of this character. We do not have to wait until the time of Domitian and Trajan for their arrival. We have only to read the book of Acts.

On the other hand, it is highly plausible that Peter, writing on the eve of those outrages against the Christians that were shortly to commence under Nero and in varying forms and degrees to spread across the Empire, was guided by the Spirit of God to forewarn and forearm the believers of Asia Minor in the tonic terms of chapter 4. Walls is justified, it seems to me, in the judgment that "The new peril is new only in degree, not in kind. Formally, 4: 12—5: 11 is best treated as a recapitulation of what has gone before, strongly reinforcing its principal lessons."[1]

2. If the epistle is one of suffering, it is also an epistle of hope. Serving as a magnificent foil for the extended notice that Peter takes of the Church's privations and persecutions is the luminous assurance he gives that history and prophecy, the past and the future, are alike in God's strong hands and that the "end" will be the revelation of His glory in the unveiling of Jesus Christ.

This is what our apostle calls a "living hope" (1: 3) in contrast to a hundred dreams and prospects that lay dead all around in the ever-dimming glow of Athens and Rome. Nor is this hope a frail match-light kept precariously aflame by anxious human effort. It is a beacon whose candlepower is produced as much by what *has* occurred as it is by what *will*

[1] *Op. cit.*, p. 51.

occur. For Peter there is an indissoluble connection between the first advent of Christ and the second, between the resurrection in which He broke the bars of death forever and the revelation in which He will consummate the triumph already achieved at the Cross and proclaimed by the empty grave. Hence He speaks in one breath of "the sufferings of Christ and the subsequent glory" (1 : 11).

Hence, also, he can declare that "the end of all things is at hand" (4 : 7). It is the perfect tense, meaning that something has already taken place which holds both the earnest and the guarantee of a future and final fulfilment. There would be little, if any, inaccuracy in translating it : "The end has begun." As Selwyn puts it : "It is not a question of the speedy occurrence of something wholly novel but of the culmination of something already known."[1] The devil is not going to be defeated. He has been defeated. It is the abandonment of his pretension to be undefeated that is yet to occur.

3. Peculiar to *I Peter* is the endlessly debated passage in chapter 3 that is often described as the Descent Into Hell (3 : 18–22). Linked with the concept of our Lord's preaching to the "spirits in prison" is the image of Noah's ark and its significance for Christian baptism. Some notion of the magnitude of the exegetical problems belonging to this passage may be gained from the fact that Dean Selwyn's immensely erudite commentary on the epistle contains a supplement in which an essay of nearly fifty pages is devoted exclusively to the linguistic, the grammatical, and the theological issues which these verses raise. The interpretation that appears most convincing to me will be indicated when we come to the exposition of chapter 3.

In Form

On two or three of the formal aspects of the epistle there is virtually unanimous agreement :

1. The *style*. The excellence of the Greek that is employed is disputed by none.

[1] *Op. cit.*, pp. 111, 112.

2. The *didactic pattern*. The ancient commentator, Oecumeniius, called *I Peter* "a teaching epistle". So it is. Yet not in the same way that some other epistles are. Where, for example, *Romans* argues, *I Peter* instructs and implores. Where *Galatians* rebukes, *I Peter* announces and appeals. The character of the letter is everywhere informed by its practical purpose.

3. The *use of "sources"*. Peter loves to quote without quotation marks! He is saturated with the Hebrew Scriptures, the Septuagint (Greek) rendering of which he likes best. As for sayings that he remembered from the lips of Jesus, they are repeatedly interwoven with his own words. The extent to which this appears to be true can be appreciated only by inspection of some such minute analysis of the evidence which may be found in Essay II of the Supplement in Selwyn's monumental work.[1]

On the other hand, several attempts, all of comparatively recent date, to discover in *I Peter* schemes or forms hitherto undetected have so far failed to carry with them a weight of evidence that compels agreement beyond a relatively small circle.

1. Dibelius has advanced the theory that the epistle is understood best as a mirror of public worship among the early Christians, its form being chiefly liturgical.

2. Perdelwitz is in partial agreement with Dibelius, but would have the liturgy confined principally, if not exclusively, to the baptismal service. This is essentially Preisker's view as well.

3. Streeter, influenced by Perdelwitz, proposed the view that the epistle falls into two parts, one a baptismal sermon and the other a pastoral letter, both produced by Aristion, the Bishop of Smyrna.

4. Beare, joining Streeter in rejecting the Petrine authorship, is less inclined to excesses of speculation, and simply

---

[1] It is the meticulous kind of research represented by the Tables in this essay that I had in mind in calling the present chapter "An Epistle Under the Microscope".

states it as his view that the letter is really "baptismal discourse, addressed to a group of recent converts".[1]

5. Cross, taking the "baptismal service" position, has re-
finements that are peculiar to his exhaustively worked-out
treatment of the case. He believes that *I Peter* records for
us the officiant's part (pastor or bishop) in a baptismal service
held on Easter Day.[2]

It remains for us to take notice of two possibilities, both of
these bearing a relation to the question of the epistle's form;
and both, it may be added, compatible with the ancient view
that Peter, with Silvanus, did indeed write it.

1. Professor C. F. D. Moule has suggested that two letters,
each containing much material that was identical, were written
simultaneously. One of them (1: 1—4: 1 with a closing greet-
ing) was addressed to the Christians in districts where persecution was bitter. The other (1: 1—2: 10; 4: 12—5: 14) was
to be delivered to believers in areas where acute trouble
was only still a threat. If so, the fusion took place without
evidence of textual disarrangement, which seems almost too
remarkable.

2. Archbishop Carrington, in his *The Primitive Christian
Catechism*, was able to convince Selwyn that the Forms in many
of the earliest Christian teachings (both sermonic and didactic),
drawn up and circulated—even while the New Testament
was in the making—appear in a variety of ways in Peter's
letter.

The fact that "form criticism" has suffered in the hands of
extremists, suffered indeed precisely as any "approach" will
suffer when *imagination* is made to do duty for *evidence*, must
not be allowed to blind us to its valid procedures and findings.

---

[1] *Ibid.*, p. 7.
[2] For the working out of this hypothesis, and evaluations of it by others,
cf. F. L. Cross, *I Peter: A Paschal Liturgy* (Mowbrays, London: 1954); F. W.
Beare, *The First Epistle of Peter*, pp. 196–202; and Andrew F. Walls in the
"Introduction" to Alan Stibbs' *The First Epistle General of Peter*, pp. 61, 62.
When scholars—a few at least—see baptism writ large over the whole epistle,
Walls' remark is worth noting: "The one place in the epistle which contains
an explicit reference to baptism is a parenthesis." Is he not right?

There is nothing either incredible or discreditable in the indications that Peter, with Silvanus, drew on a "Holiness Code" with which many of the Primitive Christians were familiar; that he borrowed ideas and phrases from a scheme of instruction for catechumens; that he adapted a sermon of his own (or perhaps one of Silvanus', who according to Acts 15: 32 was a "prophet") preached at a baptismal service; or that he incorporated into his "Christian ethics" for the guidance of believers advices whose very phrasing had become commonplace, such as *Deponentes* (a section of catechetical instruction concerned with renunciation of such iniquities as idolatry and vice), or *Subiecti* (a section concerned with Christian meekness in action, including the application of the "subordinatist" principle, of which Peter makes much in the heartland of his letter, 2: 13—3: 17), or the *Vigilate* (the necessity of watchfulness and prayer). Cannot the end-product, with all of its conscious or unconscious borrowings, be the weaving of the Holy Ghost?

After all, the image to be conjured up is not that of two drudges mechanically copying down what others have been repeating, but rather that of two kindled minds, passionate in their solicitude for troubled fellow-Christians in the towns and along the trade-routes of northern Asia Minor, fashioning a letter that they pray will lift high the hearts of the harassed and make steady the steps of the faltering.

How little, how utterly little, they realized the pricelessness of what they produced, or, better, what they let the Spirit of God within them produce! For when they had finished, they had given the Christian Church a sharper blade than ever a sword-crafter whetted, with which to be armed against all of trouble's assaults and "death's endeavour".

Of it Professor Goodspeed will say: "First Peter is one of the most moving pieces of persecution literature." Mayor will proclaim it as his feeling that no epistle in the New Testament can equal it for "sustained stateliness of rhytnm". Professor Moffatt, acknowledging that "The beautiful spirit of the pastoral shines through any translation of the Greek text", will aver that "The keynote is steady encouragement to endurance in conduct, and innocent in character".[1]

Amy Carmichael has written:

> *"Oh, there are things in the world today*
> *Would root up faith, but for Gethsemane.*
>
> *For Calvary interprets human life;*
> *No path of pain but there we meet our Lord;*
> *And all the strain, the terror and the strife*
> *Die down like waves before His peaceful word,*
> *And nowhere but beside the awful Cross,*
> *And where the olives grow along the hill,*
> *Can we accept the unexplained, the loss,*
> *The crushing agony, and hold us still."*

The lines are thoroughly Petrine.

"But if when you do right and suffer for it you take it patiently, you have God's approval. For to this you have been called, because Christ also suffered for you, leaving you an example, that you should follow in his steps" (2 : 20, 21).

And now the long, high trail is calling—the trail of those who are or, at any rate, may be

Triumphant in Trouble!

[1] This group of quotations may be found in Barclay, *The Letters of James and Peter*, pp. 164, 170.

II
THE OBLIGATIONS OF PRIVILEGE

II

THE OBLIGATIONS OF PRIVILEGE

THE OVERVIEW

Wʜᴀᴛ we are about to examine is a *letter*. Because we say the Bible has sixty-six "books", we tend to think of a precious fragment like *I Peter* as a book. It wasn't that in the eyes of its author or in the eyes of its recipients. It was an epistle. Even if we were to be persuaded by a recent theory that a substantial part of the document embodies the liturgy of a baptismal service in common use among the early Christians, it remains a fact that its literary form is that of a letter. As a letter it was dispatched and as a letter it circulated.

Let's remember, too, that in this letter the characteristic mood of the writer is that of *exhortation* and *encouragement*. Such majesty of theological discourse as you find in the letter to the Romans is not here. Such fiery sting of rebuke to heresy as you find in *Galatians* is not here. But tender pleading, fervent appeal, the loftiness of high summons—that is here. The significant and repetitive phrases (as found in a translation such as Phillips) are: "I beg you . . . I urge you."

Let's keep in mind a third thing: the Christians of Asia Minor who received this letter, whether they were Jews or Gentiles, had one thing in common, and that was *trouble*. "We may conclude," writes Walls, "that *I Peter* relates to a church that is suffering as New Testament Christians invariably did suffer. As in the Acts, their major trials came from unofficial or semi-official sources, or official sources acting *ultra vires*."[1]

The *fact* indeed is matched by the *word*; "suffer", either as

---

[1] *Ibid.*, p. 53.

noun or verb, appears prominently in each of the five chapters. When a copy of the *New English Bible* reached my hands, I put a red circle around each appearance of the word in *I Peter*. In the one hundred and five verses of the epistle there are seventeen circles. In my copy of the *Revised Standard Version* there are sixteen circles. In five instances the word is applied to the passion of our Lord. In the others it is applied to the difficulties and persecutions of the Christians. The two sufferings, His and ours, although worlds apart from one point of view, are nevertheless closely related.

This broad observation concerning the emphasis on suffering, I should add, takes no account of the different Greek words that are translated into the one English word "suffering".

And now, one more thing before we examine the letter: *an overview of the epistle as a whole.* Since, as we have noted, the dominant mood of the writer is *hortatory* and his chief approach to his readers is in the form of a series of entreaties, we don't expect a discussion that is highly organized or systematic. Yet a broad outline is discernible:

Introduction: 1: 1–12
  I. *Appeals Linked with the Privileges of the People of God:* 1: 13—2: 10
  II. *Appeals Linked with the Practices of the People of God:* 2: 11—4: 6
  III. *Appeals Linked with the Perils of the People of God:* 4: 7—5: 11
Conclusion: 5: 12–14

And now to the contents of the letter!

THE INTRODUCTION

In Rome (almost certainly) about the year 64 (very probably), with the aid of Silvanus (as acknowledged at the close), Peter begins his bracing message to his buffeted brethren far away. His introduction falls into two parts.

1. *An Address to the Believers*

This consists of an *identification* of the writer: "PETER, AN
APOSTLE OF JESUS CHRIST." Brief, simple, direct. An "apostle"
is one *sent*, as an authorized agent or representative. In the
case of the original apostles the authorization was given by the
risen Lord to those who were witnesses of His resurrection.
Hence Phillips' adoption of the title "Special Messenger". Peter
was that—despite his one-time failures. The denier has become
the defender. In the fires of Pentecost the mere bravado has
been burned out. In its place is the steadfast courage of a man
"crucified with Christ". The impetuous vacillator has become
the impregnable votary, who now takes it in hand to brace the
hearts of his Christian brothers.

The identification of the writer is followed by a *description*
of the readers: "TO THE EXILES OF THE DISPERSION IN PONTUS,
GALATIA, CAPPADOCIA, ASIA, AND BITHYNIA, CHOSEN AND
DESTINED BY GOD THE FATHER AND SANCTIFIED BY THE SPIRIT
FOR OBEDIENCE TO JESUS CHRIST AND FOR SPRINKLING WITH
HIS BLOOD" (vv. 1, 2). As to their *temporal situation*, they are
scattered pilgrims, dispersed exiles, in five areas of what was
probably northern Asia Minor, where the work of the Apostle
Paul had not extended.

As to their *spiritual status*, they are the "chosen", or "elect"
(AV), of God. We search here in vain for an explanation of the
mystery of election, but what we do get is light on how it
operated:

(*a*) This election has its *source* somewhere in the "foreknow-
ledge of God the Father". The rendering of the AV is obscured
both by the word "destined" in the RSV and "purpose" in
the NEB. It will become clear, as Peter goes on, that the same
Father-God foreknew and foreordained that He would have
the Church as His people under the new Covenant.

(*b*) This election has its *sphere* in what is suggested by the
phrase "sanctified by the Spirit". Here, apparently, is a
pregnant phrase in which is gathered up all of the divine action

through which the Church, both positionally and experimentally, both crucially and progressively, is given that separatedness and sanctity which God intends for it.

(*c*) This election has its *sign*. It is in fact a double sign: "FOR (or 'unto') OBEDIENCE TO JESUS CHRIST AND FOR SPRINKLING WITH HIS BLOOD." The sign and proof of being among the "elect" is not an empty prating of how secure we are once we have believed, but rather how sensitive we are to the principle and practice of obedience to the Saviour we have trusted. To be sure, our security never is *grounded* in our obedience, but it is signified thereby as being the very intention of God in bestowing His favour upon us. This obedience, moreover, is made possible by a continuous reliance upon the merits of the Saviour, the "sprinkling of his blood".

Thus we reach the *benediction* of the writer upon the readers: "MAY GRACE (as the *fount* of your salvation) AND PEACE (as the *fruit* of your salvation) BE MULTIPLIED TO YOU."

2. *An Ascription to God*

This is the second part of the introduction. It covers the next seven verses, commencing with a burst of praise: "BLESSED BE THE GOD AND FATHER OF OUR LORD JESUS CHRIST!" The Greek word for "blessed" is one from which we derive the English word "eulogy". So Professor Kenneth Wuest, in his *First Peter in the Greek New Testament*, renders it, "Let the God and Father of our Lord Jesus Christ be eulogized."

Our way of eulogizing is sharply different from the Bible's way. We eulogize dead men (usually at a funeral); the Bible eulogizes the living God.

Peter says, in effect, "Brothers in the faith, I know your troubles, and I am going to talk to you about them, but before I come to this I want you to join me in a doxology."

What are the strains of it?

(*a*) For one thing, he would lead them in praise to God for *the prospect they may cherish beyond all their torture and troubles*: "BY HIS GREAT MERCY WE HAVE BEEN BORN ANEW TO A LIVING

HOPE THROUGH THE RESURRECTION OF JESUS CHRIST FROM THE DEAD, AND TO AN INHERITANCE WHICH IS IMPERISHABLE, UNDEFILED, AND UNFADING, KEPT IN HEAVEN FOR YOU" (vv. 3, 4). Let's learn to distinguish between persons who are temperamentally optimistic and persons who are theologically hopeful. By "theologically" I do not mean "theoretically". I mean persons whose confidence in the eternal brightness that lies beyond all death and all doom is firmly based on what God has revealed in His Holy Word and on the personal experience of His transforming life and love which they have found in Christ. The resurrected Lord, in whom they have trusted, has struck them through with a newness that is like birth. Could a *dead* Christ give such life as this?

Nor is that all. This risen Saviour has engaged Himself to provide for the sons and daughters of faith a heavenly inheritance which may be thought of as a kind of guarded deposit whose riches are awaiting us when our often trouble-filled pilgrimage here has run its course. Keep your hope-lit eyes on that "inheritance", Peter would say. It is "imperishable": no termites, no moulding, no decaying! It is "undefiled": no sin will ever stain it, no rebellion will ever rock it! It is "unfading": its beauty will be forever undiminished, its charm forever enchanting!

Israel's "inheritance" in the Promised Land was not "imperishable", or, as the Greek word may be rendered, "unravagable": it was invaded and ravaged again and again. It was not "undefiled": Jehovah's repeated complaint was that apostate Israel polluted the land with her idolatries. It was not "unfading": the magnificence of the temple was blotted out, the glory of Zion went into eclipse.

But of the Church's "inheritance" in heaven this will never be true. For in the ultimate sense Christ Himself, the Christ of glory, is the everlasting possession of His people. In that day when Christ is revealed in advent splendour, when He appears, and when the Church, as St. Paul would say, shall "appear with Him in glory" (Colossians 3 : 4), the whole Church will cry, as the Psalmist does in Psalm 16: 5: "The Lord is the portion of mine inheritance."

A bereaved wife, after listening to some verses I had quoted at the funeral of her husband, requested a copy of them. It was obvious that the hope the poet describes had found a voice in her hoping heart:

> *"How beautiful to be with God,*
> *When earth is fading like a dream,*
> *And from this mist-encircled shore*
> *We launch upon the unknown stream:*
> *Then let it fade, this dream of earth,*
> *When I have done my life-work here,*
> *Or long, or short, as seemeth best—*
> *What matters so God's will appears.*
> *I will not fear to launch my bark*
> *Upon the darkly rolling flood,*
> *'Tis but to pierce the mist—and then*
> *How beautiful to be with God!"* [1]

Such is the prospect, declares Peter, that is "kept in heaven for you". The prospect that may be cherished beyond all of your troubles!

(*b*) Listen now to a second note of thanks that belongs to this chord of praise! Peter would lead them in gratitude to God *for the power that they may experience in the midst of all their troubles:* "WHO BY GOD'S POWER ARE GUARDED THROUGH FAITH FOR A SALVATION READY TO BE REVEALED IN THE LAST TIME" (v. 5).

"Guarded" is a good word, but let's not surrender the word "kept" as we have it in the Authorized Version. In the preceding verse we have been told that our "inheritance" is being "kept" for us in heaven; in this verse we have the counterpart of that truth: we are being "kept" amid the perils and difficulties of this testing, tumultuous world through which we must pass.

[1] James L. Christensen, *Funeral Services* (Fleming H. Revell, New York: 1959), quoted from *Wayside Altar*, poem by W. Halsey Smith.

What over-reaches and underlies both of these keepings is nothing less than "the power of God".

"Kept by the power of God!" A tremendous phrase! Who could thrill to it more than Peter? He who once tried to keep himself! Impetuous and self-reliant, full of zeal toward his Master, he was sure that, though others might not hold to their loyalty to Him, he would. Then the sickening failure . . . the dark denial . . . the bitter tears . . . the tender recovery!

But even that was not enough. Something happened to Peter that gave him such a knowledge of God's kind of power working at man's level of need as he had never known before. He got the clue to it from the risen Jesus: "Ye shall receive power when the Holy Spirit has come upon you" (Acts 1: 8). He got the confirmation of it on the Day of Pentecost, when he (along with others of his friends) was mightily "filled with the Holy Spirit".

Kept by God's power, Peter is no longer the denier: he is the declarer. The discovery that this was God's gift came to him in a flash, but the discipline of unceasing surrender and trust had to be maintained in a moment-by-moment communion with power's great Source.

If we could only see this! And, with Peter, live there! No matter how difficult or diabolical or disastrous the circumstances, some people are always being "kept". Noah and his family in the pre-Flood wickedness, Joseph amid the wiles and witcheries of a heathen house and a designing woman, Daniel hard set by the voluptuous allurements of Babylon, Paul surrounded by angry mobs and haughty monarchs— somehow the "power of God" garrisoned them. They were kept. And that "somehow", once we know God's word on the matter, becomes more specific: it is "through faith". It is quiet, unshakable, unyielding confidence in the presence, resources, and utter faithfulness of the Lord who by His Spirit lives within us.

This is a trust which, renouncing self and its pitiful inadequacies, rests down upon the Christ who wears the insignia of power, the marks of the Cross and the Empty Tomb.

Of this faith it has been said:

> "*Her feet are firmly planted on the Rock,*
> *Then 'midst the wildest storms she stands undaunted,*
> *Nor quails before the loudest thunder-shock;*
> *She knows Omnipotence has heard her prayer,*
> *Cries, it shall be answered sometime, somewhere.*"

(*c*) Listen once more as this soaring eulogy fills out its chord of thanks. Peter would have his readers join him in praise *for the profit they may derive from all their troubles:* "IN THIS YOU REJOICE, THOUGH NOW FOR A LITTLE WHILE YOU MAY HAVE TO SUFFER VARIOUS TRIALS, SO THAT THE GENUINENESS OF YOUR FAITH, MORE PRECIOUS THAN GOLD WHICH THOUGH PERISHABLE IS TESTED BY FIRE, MAY REDOUND TO PRAISE AND GLORY AND HONOUR AT THE REVELATION OF JESUS CHRIST" (vv. 6, 7).

There are three Christian axioms we ought to know by heart:

1. *Trouble is something we should take for granted.* It belongs. Some kinds of suffering belong to life in general. They come alike to Christian and non-Christian. Other varieties of trouble are brought upon us by our discipleship to Christ. In any case, trouble is part of the scheme of things for the Christian. After what our Lord endured, the disciple should not say: "I never thought this would happen to *me*!"

2. *Trouble is something that does not last.* Peter's descriptive phrase is "a little while". True, that means much longer in the case of some trials than it does in others. "This too will pass" is nevertheless a sensible attitude to assume. Most of our troubles pass so quickly that when we look back on them we are astonished that they form so small a segment of our lives.

3. *Trouble is something that should not be wasted.* It is not good in itself, but it can be turned to good. Not to convert it into something valuable is to waste it. Phillips, in his paraphrase, makes this passage read: "At present you are temporarily

harassed by all kinds of trials and temptations. This is no accident—it happens to prove your faith, which is infinitely more valuable than gold." Some years ago, in one of his books for daily reading, Dr. E. Stanley Jones wrote, as the "Affirmation for the Day": "Grief comes to all, sours some, sweetens others. I shall use it to sweeten my spirit." Note the verb—"use".

"Psychiatrists," says Karl Menninger, "realize from clinical experience what poets have proclaimed in inspired verse, that to retreat into the loneliness of one's own soul (in time of suffering) is to surrender one's claim upon life." From the highest Christian point of view, I would amend the last part of the sentence: It is to "surrender one's claim *upon the Christ who gives mastery over all of life*—suffering included!"

Now, says Peter, this "proved residue of your faith", as Professor Griffith Thomas translated it, will bring in the end a magnificent reward: "IT IS PLANNED TO BRING YOU PRAISE AND HONOUR AND GLORY IN THE DAY WHEN JESUS CHRIST REVEALS HIMSELF" (v. 7). A threefold reward: (1) He will commend you; (2) He will be honoured to acknowledge you; (3) He will share His everlasting glory with you.

Give praise, then, to the Lord, who, though your mortal eyes have never seen Him, is none the less the object of your adoring love: "WITHOUT HAVING SEEN HIM YOU LOVE HIM; THOUGH YOU DO NOT NOW SEE HIM YOU BELIEVE IN HIM AND REJOICE WITH UNUTTERABLE AND EXALTED JOY. AS THE OUTCOME OF YOUR FAITH YOU OBTAIN THE SALVATION OF YOUR SOULS" (vv. 8, 9).

The faith that accepts salvation *becomes* the love that adores the Saviour. Here and now the Saviour offers release from sin's guilt and bondage. Here and now faith, which someone has defined as "pure receptivity", closes with the offer, takes it, rests in it. But this, as Peter points out, is no impersonal transaction, like doing business with your bank by post through someone who is known anonymously as the "mail teller". This is flinging open your personality to the wooings of a Lover and finding that your response to the love He bestows is a ravishing, wordless, redeeming wonder. So Havergal sings:

> *"I love, I love my Master,*
> *I will not go out free;*
> *For He is my Redeemer;*
> *He paid the price for me.*
> *I would not leave His service,*
> *It is so sweet and blest;*
> *And in the weariest moments*
> *He gives the truest rest.*
>
> *"I would not halve my service,*
> *His only it must be:*
> *His only, who so loved me,*
> *And gave Himself for me;*
> *Rejoicing and adoring,*
> *Henceforth my song shall be.*
> *I love, I love my Master,*
> *I will not go out free."*

So another exclaims:

> *"How can I choose but love Thee, God's dear son,*
> *O Jesus, loveliest and most loving One?*
> *Were there no heaven to gain, no hell to flee,*
> *For what Thou art alone I must love thee."* [1]

The key words in verses 8 and 9 are participles and adjectives:

(*a*) "Believing" (here the King James is more faithful than the RSV) is in the present tense, descriptive of continual or habitual activity. Trust, and keep on trusting!

(*b*) "Receiving" (again following the AV), "a present participle in the middle voice, expressing the idea of 'acquiring for oneself' in personal appropriation and enjoyment." [2] In

---

[1] Quoted by James Stewart in *The Gates of New Life* (Charles Scribner's Sons, New York: 1940), p. 126; (T. & T. Clarke, Edinburgh).

[2] Alan M. Stibbs, *The First Epistle General of Peter* (Wm. B. Eerdmans Publishing Company, Grand Rapids: 1959), p. 80.

the life of habitual trust the merits of the Saviour become verifiably and enjoyably ours. We gratefully cherish a forgiveness that really releases us and a love that really kindles us.

(c) "Unspeakable", as applied to joy, and "full" as applied to glory. Beyond all our ability to put it in words our joy in Christ is lit up now with as much of the glory of heaven as our present frailties will allow.

In this summons to "eulogize" God—even when trouble is knocking us about—Peter has brought together, in a living blend, the *present* and the *future* tenses of "salvation". "WE HAVE BEEN BORN ANEW," he cries in verse 3. Here is salvation presently obtained (v. 9). But in verse 5 he has spoken of "A SALVATION READY TO BE REVEALED IN THE LAST TIME". St. Paul held an identical view, for in Romans 13: 11 he assures those already saved that "salvation is nearer to us now than when we first believed". In a special note that he has on the double meaning which Peter gives to "Salvation", Dean Selwyn remarks: "The process of salvation was begun at conversion; but it was governed then, as it is governed now, by the End to which it looks and which will only be accomplished in 'the last time' when God's purpose for all things is complete."[1]

This allusion to the vastness of the redemption that is ours in Christ leads Peter to give his readers a kind of addendum to his introduction, in which he brings forward both prophets and angels as witnesses to the sheer wonder of the total salvation God has given through His Son:

"THE PROPHETS WHO PROPHESIED OF THE GRACE THAT WAS TO BE YOURS SEARCHED AND INQUIRED ABOUT THIS SALVATION; THEY INQUIRED WHAT PERSON OR TIME WAS INDICATED BY THE SPIRIT OF CHRIST WITHIN THEM WHEN PREDICTING THE SUFFERINGS OF CHRIST AND THE SUBSEQUENT GLORY. IT WAS REVEALED TO THEM THAT THEY WERE SERVING NOT THEMSELVES BUT YOU, IN THE THINGS WHICH HAVE NOW BEEN ANNOUNCED TO YOU BY THOSE WHO PREACHED THE GOOD NEWS TO YOU THROUGH THE

[1] Selwyn, *The First Epistle of Peter* (Macmillan and Company, New York: 1946), p. 252.

HOLY SPIRIT SENT FROM HEAVEN, THINGS INTO WHICH ANGELS LONG TO LOOK" (vv. 10–12).

Expositors have had their struggles with parts of this passage. Into the intricacies of the problems we shall not enter. Let four things be gathered, in sum, from what Peter says:

(a) The Prophets, inspired by the Holy Spirit (who is indeed the "Spirit of Christ"), foreannounced that God's Christ must suffer. (Dean Selwyn's contention that these were prophets of the Apostolic Church, as well as prophets of the Old Testament, seems to me to be unconvincing.)

(b) They further prophesied that for Him this path of suffering would lead to incalculable "glories". The Greek is plural, in reference, we may suppose, to the *manifold* results of the Cross: Resurrection, Ascension, Pentecost, the Church and its World Mission, the Second Advent. The rendering of the *New English Bible* is attractive: "THE SUFFERINGS IN STORE FOR CHRIST AND THE SPLENDOURS TO FOLLOW." "Glory," however, remains a richer word than "splendour".

(c) They foresaw, without fully comprehending, that towering high among these gracious consequences of the Cross would be the inclusion of the Gentiles within the compass of God's redeeming mercy and their participation in the fellowship of the Church of His Son. The obvious link between verse 10 of chapter 1 and verse 10 of chapter 2 has not been missed by most expositors.

(d) So unutterably grand is all of this—the mysterious design of God in the Cross of Christ—that angels, baffled, long for clearer understanding of it.

> "But the high mysteries of Thy name
> An angels grasp transcend;
> Thy Father only—glorious claim—
> The Son can comprehend:
> Worthy, O Lamb of God, art Thou
> That every knee to Thee should bow." [1]

[1] J. Conder, "Thou Art the Everlasting Word" from the *Keswick Hymn-book* (Marshall, Morgan, & Scott, London) No. 314.

So Peter's introduction ends. Its soaring style has well matched its theological sweep.

Now for matters more mundane—though even these are never far removed from the celestial light by which alone they can be managed!

I APPEALS LINKED WITH THE PRIVILEGES OF THE PEOPLE OF GOD: 1: 13—2: 10

The characteristic note of bracing exhortation is struck in verse 13: "THEREFORE GIRD UP YOUR MINDS, BE SOBER." "You must therefore be like men stripped for action, perfectly self-controlled," is the colourful rendering of the *New English Bible*. Trouble-encircled they may be, but they are to be "calm and collected in spirit" (Wuest translation).

This, when spelled out, will be found to require three things:

1. *Live Steadfastly—in Hope:* 1: 13.
"SET YOUR HOPE FULLY UPON THE GRACE THAT IS COMING TO YOU AT THE REVELATION OF JESUS CHRIST" (v. 13).

"Set your hope!"

The grammatical form is an aorist imperative, which Peter uses repeatedly to strengthen the force of an ordinary present tense. To get the full vigour of Peter's address we need to give it some such amplification as: "Once for all, focus your hope unalterably, without doubting or desponding, upon the grace that is being brought to you at the revelation of Jesus Christ."

Because the verb translated "coming" or "being brought" is in the present tense, some expositors, including Luther and Bengel, refer this to the progressively unfolding hope of the Christian in the life he *now* lives, in which Christ is daily revealed to him. These respected names to the contrary, one feels that the context calls for an interpretation that looks ahead to the unveiling of the returning Lord. But then, it needs to be kept in mind that "hope" and "grace" and "glory" are words that Peter sees in two dimensions at one and the same time. They have potent meaning *both* for the present and for the future.

As Selwyn observes, "Our author . . . regards the object of hope as already virtually possessed."[1] Or as Maclaren puts it: "The 'grace' is not contrasted with the 'glory', but is another name for the glory."[2]

We make a mistake if we imagine that the gayly gilded civilization of Rome, with all of its poetry and art and political finesse, was lit up with any great and abiding hopes. After citing a particularly pessimistic quotation from Sophocles, Dr. C. E. B. Cranfield, of Durham University, remarks that over the classical Graeco-Roman civilization "death reigned as king of terrors, spoiling men's enjoyment of the present with the intruding thought of the future, so that life could seem a gift not worth receiving, and death in infancy preferable to growing up to the conscious anticipation of having to die".[3]

For the disciples of Jesus, His resurrection had blasted that sort of despair into irrecoverable bits, and, in its place, had set aflame the unquenchable hope that

> "*Surely He cometh, and a thousand voices*
> *Shout to the saints, and to the deaf are dumb;*
> *Surely He cometh, and the earth rejoices,*
> *Glad in His coming who hath sworn: I come!*"[4]

Now, says Peter, hold this hope unwaveringly. Neither the "hope to the end" of the Authorized Version nor the plain "fix your hopes" of the *New English Bible* does full justice to the Greek. Selwyn suggests an idiom to bring out the force of it: "Give yourself to this hope up to the hilt." No reservation, no holding back! Then you will never be shaken by the mordant pessimism of an H. G. Wells, who long ago wrote of life:

1. *Op. cit.*, p. 140.
2. Cf. Alexander Maclaren, *Expositions of Holy Scripture;* 1 *Peter*, Vol. 16 (Eerdmans).
3. *Op. cit.*, p. 37.
4. F. W. H. Myers, "Hark What a Sound" from the *Keswick Hymn-book* (Marshall, Morgan, & Scott, London) No. 377.

"The experiment will be over, the crystals gone, dissolving down the wastepipe." On the contrary, you will know that beyond earth's farthest, dimmest horizon there is *another*, whose bright circumference is never darkened by a setting sun.

2. *Live Sensitively—in Holiness* 1:14–21.

Charles Erdman rightly remarks that holiness is the supreme thought of the paragraph.[1] But the logic of Peter's appeal will appear in full force only after we have discovered the privileged status that God in His grace has conferred upon His redeemed people. It is threefold: (1) that of *children* (v. 14); (2) that of *pilgrims* (v. 17); and that of *freedmen* (v. 18).

a. First of all, be sensitive to your *status*! "AS OBEDIENT CHILDREN, DO NOT BE CONFORMED TO THE PASSIONS OF YOUR FORMER IGNORANCE, BUT AS HE WHO HATH CALLED YOU IS HOLY, BE HOLY YOURSELVES IN ALL YOUR CONDUCT." This may be paraphrased: "You are children in the Father's family, and the likeness to Him which you are to bear speaks of holiness."

Now on to verse 17: "CONDUCT YOURSELVES WITH FEAR THROUGHOUT THE TIME OF YOUR EXILE." Paraphrase it thus: "You are pilgrims in transit, and the Homeland that calls you speaks of holiness."

Verse 18: "YOU KNOW THAT YOU WERE RANSOMED FROM THE FUTILE WAYS INHERITED FROM YOUR FATHERS." A free paraphrase might be: "You are slaves made free, and the 'precious blood' that purchased you speaks of holiness."

The argument, you see, keeps moving from *identity* to *responsibility*, from *calling* to *conduct*, from *privilege* to *obligation*.

We must examine this more closely.

(1.) *Consider the "children" status and the obligation arising therefrom:* "AS OBEDIENT CHILDREN." Neither the AV nor the ASV is quite as expressive as the Revised Version, which renders this phrase "children of obedience". The Greek, as one scholar has pointed out, is best understood as a Hebraism

---

[1] Cf. Charles R. Erdman, *The General Epistles* (Westminster Press, Philadelphia), p. 60.

with overtones that describe not merely children of God who are obedient but those whose very life is lived out of the "womb" of obedience, who are given over to its habitual expression and practice. It is the opposite of St. Paul's phrase in Ephesians 2: 2, where he speaks of "children of disobedience".

Note the contrasting affinities, one of which is to be decisively shattered, while the other is to be profoundly shared: "DO NOT BE CONFORMED TO THE PASSIONS OF YOUR FORMER IGNORANCE, BUT AS HE WHO HAS CALLED YOU IS HOLY, BE HOLY YOUR-SELVES." "Not fashioning yourselves according to," is the familiar translation of the Authorized. The Greek verb for "to fashion" speaks of that which is superficial, transitory. In the days when you were without the knowledge of God you followed those fickle fancies of men. Let that pattern of living no longer dominate you.

On the other hand, your new standard of living is nothing less than God himself in his shining, stainless holiness. So Peter argues. So, too, he appeals. For, after all, the infinite and independent source and ground of all holiness, goodness, and truth are in God himself.

Why should the Bible have so much to say about Holiness—under the Old Covenant and under the New? The reasons are numerous, but they all come down to this in finality: God is holy and the passion of his heart, held in poignant focus at Calvary, is the creation of a family of children who will in fact be like him.

Readers of Dietrich Bonhoeffer's *The Cost of Discipleship* will know of his bold thesis that much of Christendom has long since subsided into a misunderstanding, and consequently a misuse, of the concept of grace and the doctrine of "justifi-cation by faith". The deviation, which he passionately believed to be disastrous, is tersely described in a sentence which, slightly varied, he repeats many times: "We have perverted the doctrine of the justification of the *sinner* into the justification of the *sin*."

As a consequence, says Bonhoeffer, Christendom has been flooded—and fouled—with what he calls "cheap grace". This, in the final resort, is man justifying himself rather than penitently taking God's justification of him in Christ and, with it, the costly implications of the holy obedience to which it leads. "Costly grace" is the real thing, as contrasted with "cheap grace".

Bonhoeffer is right. God is not in the business of justifying sin. He is in the fabulously gracious business of justifying the sinner in order that the justified sinner may in sanctification glorify Him, the redeeming Father who gave his Son for us.

The question inevitably arises: a *holy* Christian? *How?* *When?* The questions have propriety. They also have peril. We want answers that are even tidier than the New Testament. The answers we attempt send us off on old scents, long familiar to the theological hounds: "second blessing?" "suppression?" "counteraction?" "eradication?" "holiness movements?" "holiness conventions?" The whole thing has been crammed into a "mixed bag" of teaching and witness: truth, half-truth, and error; prejudice, bigotry, and confusion; unbelief masquerading as humility on the one hand, and Pharisaism wearing the guise of piety on the other.

In some respects the New Testament is like Nature before science has taken hold of it to analyse and utilize it. It is vast, prodigious, hugely potential, and often paradoxical. So it is with the concept of holiness as rooted in God and communicated to His children:

It is gift and it is growth.

It casts out sin, yet leaves the heart of the one so cleansed unceasingly sure both of unworthiness and of disparity between it and the vision of God's perfection.

It is the heritage of all the children of God, and as such admits of no degrees, yet becomes the effective possession of the Father's children who bow to the totality of its claim and submit to the boundless vitality of the sanctifying Spirit within them.

It allows both for the assertion that all Christians are

"sanctified" and for the apostolic prayer in behalf of Christians; "May the God of peace himself sanctify you wholly."

It requires the categorical denial that sonship in the family of God carries exemption from temptation or removes the possibility of sinning.

It calls for the equally categorical assertion that grace does much more than save us *in* sinning: its intention is to save us *from* sinning, not to *modify* the carnal mind but to *crucify* it.

God must weary of our doctrinal involutions no less than our practical evasions. On any scheme known to theology—whether of *terms* or of *concepts*, whether Calvinist, Lutheran, or Arminian—we doddering, defaulting, defeated Christians would be driven to our knees, driven to the Cross, driven to Pentecost, if only we took with passionate seriousness this inviolable claim of the Father, "You shall be holy, for I am holy."

(2.) *Consider next our "pilgrim" status and the obligation that arises from it.*

"AND IF YOU INVOKE AS FATHER HIM WHO JUDGES EACH ONE IMPARTIALLY ACCORDING TO HIS DEEDS, CONDUCT YOURSELVES WITH FEAR THROUGHOUT THE TIME OF YOUR EXILE" (v. 17). The controlling part of this sentence is: "conduct yourselves with fear" (or "awe" as the *New English Bible* has it). But the suggestive segment of the sentence is: "the time of your exile."

In a little book called *The Christian Mission Today* Bishop Lesslie Newbigin makes this observation:

"*It belongs to the very nature of the Gospel that Christians are strangers and pilgrims on the earth. Properly speaking the Church is always in a colonial situation—as St. Paul told the Philippians. The fact that it has often appeared rather as a colony of some white race than as a colony of heaven is part of our present problem. But in finding ways of escape from the wrong kind of colonialism we must not lose the true foreign-ness of the Church. The Church can never be wholly at home in the world, and the fact that in its life and mission it deliberately and systematically transgresses the boundaries of nation and culture is an indispensable symbol and instrument of its supernatural calling."*

So speaking, Bishop Newbigin strikes an authentic New Testament note too often muted in the muddled, maudlin "Christianity" of our time.

Do you really belong to the people of God? asks Peter, in effect. If you do, you are pilgrims in exile, and the Homeland that beckons you speaks of that holiness which is begun here in order that you may be no stranger to the atmosphere of heaven.

Being a pilgrim is not the same thing as being a tramp. A tramp is aimless, destinationless. A pilgrim knows where he is going. The people of God, we are told in the Epistle to the Hebrews, are those who freely acknowledge that they are "strangers and exiles on the earth". Now note what follows: "For people who speak thus make it clear that they are seeking a homeland" (11 : 13, 14). This is clearly understood by Peter. It is not, however, his point of insistence in verse 17. His chief contention here is that there must be an evident consistency between the character of the lives we lead in our pilgrim state and the character of the Homeland to which we are moving. It must be seen that the Father-God to whom we pray is none other than "Our Father who art in Heaven". He is, moreover, both a merciful and judging Father.

Two things, according to Peter, may be said about the Father's judging action in the life of His children : it is *immediate* ("he who judges", with present tense noteworthy), and it is *impartial* ("who judges their actions without the slightest favouritism", so paraphrases Phillips).

By "immediate" I mean the here-and-now, continuous judgment of the Father-Judge as He tenderly, faithfully watches over us in our behaviour as His children. "Now," cries Alexander Maclaren, "do not run away with the notion that the Apostle is speaking here of that Great White Throne and the future judgment. . . . That is a solemn thought, but it is not Peter's thought here. . . . The conception is brought out of a continuous divine judgment running along, all through a man's life, side by side with his work." Maclaren then speaks of "the little spurts of bad temper", the "little gusts of worldliness", the "sting of pride", which we want to regard lightly but which He assesses and reproves. From which, let it be added, only He can deliver us!

Our privilege is clear: pilgrims of God. Our obligation is likewise clear: a day-by-day conduct, full of holy awe, with no forgetting that here on earth we are being judged by heaven's light.

(3.) *Consider, finally, our status as "freedmen" and the obligation arising from it.* The key words are: "YOU KNOW THAT YOU WERE RANSOMED FROM THE FUTILE WAYS INHERITED FROM YOUR FATHERS, NOT WITH PERISHABLE THINGS SUCH AS SILVER OR GOLD, BUT WITH THE PRECIOUS BLOOD OF CHRIST."

"Ransomed!" The Authorized Version reads "redeemed". The *New English Bible* draws it out into three words: "bought your freedom." Each is an attempt to say what the Greek word signified, which, as one Greek scholar put it, means "to set free by the payment of a ransom".

"Christians," says Professor Alan Stibbs in the Tyndale Commentary series, "need to remember that, like the Israelites whom God brought out of Egypt, they have been rescued from bondage." Here, certainly, is a clue to Peter's meaning. Follow it.

(*a*) Let's put it this way: for enslaved Israel "Egypt" was something to be *redeemed from*! In Peter's thinking, all men, being sinners, are fettered "Israelites" needing to be set free. What is their slavery? Drink, you may say. Or tobacco. Or gambling. But all this is superficial. The real bondage lies deeper. Scripture makes it plain that we are in a prison-cell of alienation from God. It is our estrangement and rootlessness that are echoed in Augustine's famous cry: "Thou hast made us for Thyself, and our souls are restless till they rest in Thee!" And there is no jail-break for any of us by the naked stroke of our strengthless hands.

Now, compound this bondage of a separation from God with the coils of a twisted self (a self tortured into the ugly shapes of conceit, and fear, and contentment with false values), and you have a slavery which is too terrible and tyrannical for any but God to break.

(*b*) Let's put Peter's next thought in this fashion—for Israel, enslaved in Egypt, the blood was something to be *redeemed by*! The Exodus narrative is readily recalled: "The blood shall be a sign for you, upon the houses where you are; and when I see the blood, I will pass over you" (Exodus 12: 13). It was to be a lamb's blood. It was to be, in effect, deliverance blood—the price and proof of the freedom God in mercy was giving them.

In the leap to the larger meaning, Peter carries us with him as he proclaims the unmatched price of the sinner's redemption: "NOT WITH PERISHABLE THINGS SUCH AS SILVER AND GOLD, BUT THE PRECIOUS BLOOD OF CHRIST, LIKE THAT OF A LAMB WITHOUT BLEMISH OR SPOT" (vv. 18, 19).

(*c*) What we are redeemed *from* is something grim—the whole futility of sin. What we are redeemed *by* is something glorious —the atoning blood of the Saviour. Add one thing more: what we are *redeemed to* is something godlike—"AS HE WHO CALLED YOU IS HOLY, BE HOLY YOURSELVES IN ALL YOUR CONDUCT" (v. 15).

Thus Peter has amplified the injunction to live sensitively in holiness by calling, first of all, for sensitivity to our *status*.

b. He next calls for sensitivity to our *Saviour*. The reference to the "precious blood of Christ" in verse 19 leads the apostle to say of Him, "HE WAS DESTINED BEFORE THE FOUNDATION OF THE WORLD BUT WAS MADE MANIFEST AT THE END OF THE TIMES FOR YOUR SAKE. THROUGH HIM YOU HAVE CONFIDENCE IN GOD, WHO RAISED HIM FROM THE DEAD AND GAVE HIM GLORY, SO THAT YOUR FAITH AND HOPE ARE IN GOD" (vv. 20, 21).

Here are three things to remember, says Peter:

(1.) The Redeemer and his role in what God has *designed*: "HE WAS DESTINED BEFORE THE FOUNDATION OF THE WORLD" (v. 20). Or, as Phillips has it: "God chose him to fulfil this part (the part of 'the unblemished and unstained Lamb of sacrifice') before the world was founded." Predestination is always mysterious. Predestination can be so presented that it is mischievous. But predestination, in any case, is something that is solidly there in the vast structure of the Christian gospel. God is not first Creator and then, of sudden and belated necessity, Redeemer. He is the Redeemer-Creator, whose Son is somehow "the lamb slain from the foundation of the world" (Revelation 13:8). On the divine side, Calvary is not an act of desperation: it is an act of design.

(2.) The Redeemer and his role in what history has *disclosed*: "HE . . . WAS MADE MANIFEST AT THE END OF THE TIMES FOR YOUR SAKE" (v. 20). What has been purposed by God in eternity has been revealed by God in history: the Redeemer has come. His coming, moreover, is in some very real sense the consummating event for which ages and generations have been in waiting. The Incarnation (generally) and the Atonement (specifically) form an end and a beginning—an end of the preparation, a beginning of the realization. As Hebrews 9:26 has it: "But as it is, he has appeared once for all at the end of the age to put away sin by the sacrifice of himself." Stibbs therefore is warranted in saying, by way of comment on this phrase: "The Christian dispensation, the point and period in history of Christ's coming, is here regarded as the climax and consummation of the previous age."

And all of this richly redemptive revelation, cries Peter, is "for your sakes"—you who, whether Gentiles or Jews, were caught in this massive web of futility which is the estranged and enslaved human family.

(3.) The Redeemer and his role in what the Church has *declared*—and must declare: "THROUGH HIM YOU HAVE CONFIDENCE IN GOD, WHO RAISED HIM FROM THE DEAD AND GAVE HIM GLORY, SO THAT YOUR FAITH AND HOPE ARE IN GOD" (v. 21). A crucified but unresurrected Jesus is no Redeemer. What gives us a Gospel is that the Cross is as bereft of its victim as is the tomb.

"There are," says Edward Rogers, "forms of most earnest
and devoted evangelical preaching and theological writing which
convey the impression that somehow the Crucifixion has over-
shadowed the Resurrection and that the whole purpose of God
in Christ was completed at Calvary. The truth, which is obscured only at grave spiritual peril, is that the Crucifixion
cannot be interpreted and understood save in the light of the
Resurrection."[1]

The connection between this stress on our Lord's resurrection
and the appeal for holy living should be clear. The Peter of the
Four Gospels felt the tug of holiness, as he saw it in Jesus, but
lacked the power to rise to it. The Peter of the Acts, on the
other hand, was always linking the resurrection of Jesus with
the victorious adequacy which had now become the possession
of the Spirit-filled Church. With sheer wonder in their eyes,
men looked at the hundred and twenty disciples on the Day
of Pentecost. Whence this courage? This fluency? This
freedom? This authority? They could but ask, "What meaneth
this?"

Peter, replying, went straight back to the resurrection.
There was the *demonstration* of God's victory over the powers
of hell. Then he went back only a step, to the filling of the
Holy Spirit that had just come to the Church. Here indeed was
the *communication* of this power to the people of God. Putting
the two together, Peter cried, with all the passionate assurance
of his now invincible spirit: "This Jesus God raised up, and of
that we are all witnesses. Being therefore exalted at the right
hand of God, and having received from the Father the promise
of the Holy Spirit, he has poured out this which you see and
hear" (Acts 2: 32, 33).

It is this which leads him to say to the Christians who will
soon be reading this letter: Live sensitively in holiness; and,
remembering your status as "children", as "pilgrims", as
"freedmen", remember also that your conquering Redeemer,

[1] Cf. Edward Rogers, *That They Might Have Life* (Channel Press, New
York: 1959), p. 10.

sin's master and death's destroyer, will enable you to bring your conduct into line with the holy purpose for which God has redeemed you.

Perseus, among the ancients, speaks of those who are "numbed with vice", and he says of the guilty: "Let them see virtue, and pine that they have lost her forever."[1] The *vision* of virtue was not lacking among the pagans; it was the *victory* of virtue which they could neither foresee nor experience. Only the resurrection faith of surrendered Christians can fill the gap between the two.

3. *Live Sincerely—in Harmony:* 1 : 22—2 : 3.

Christian harmony, it will be seen, has (1) its *essentials* and (2) its *enemies*.

1. Take the essentials, whose nub is found in the appeal, "LOVE ONE ANOTHER EARNESTLY FROM THE HEART" (v. 22). Consider:

(i) The twofold obligation with respect to this fellowship of brotherly love: "HAVING PURIFIED YOUR SOULS BY YOUR OBEDIENCE TO THE TRUTH FOR A SINCERE LOVE OF THE BRETHREN, LOVE ONE ANOTHER EARNESTLY FROM THE HEART" (v. 22).

In the phrase "a sincere love of the brethren" we have an echo of a Greek word for "love" that suggests fondness, congeniality, a "liking" for one another that springs from "alikeness". After all, we are, as previously noted, children of the one Father, members of the one family. Our "obedience to the truth" has this kind of familial affection for its aim and end.

At the same time the realities of life within the household of God are such that we find ourselves saying, alas, all too frequently, "But he is such a difficult man to get on with," or, "She is such an unattractive person."

What to do?

[1] Quoted by William Barclay in *The Promise of the Spirit* (The Epworth Press, London : 1960), p. 92.

Read the rest of the sentence: "Love one another earnestly from the heart."

"But this," you say, "is merely repeating the former clause." It sounds like this, but it is not. Here the Greek word for love is the higher, stronger one. It is *agape*. It is this word that William Barclay has in mind when, in his book *The Promise of the Spirit*, he says: "Christian love is not an emotional thing, with the ebb and flow that all emotional things must have. Christian love is that undefeatable good will which nothing can change to bitterness or hate."

The adverb that qualifies this love is "fervently" in the Authorized Version, "earnestly" in the Revised Standard. The word so translated means literally "at full stretch", or, as Stibbs suggests, "at full intensity".

How are these two aspects of love related? In two ways: (*a*) love as *agape* will save love as *philos* (that is, as mutual fondness) from deteriorating into selfish attachment; and (*b*) love as *agape* will help create or enhance love as *philos* by impelling us to serve the interests or endure the rudenesses of those whom we should otherwise ignore or resent.

Love as *agape* is both a gift and a discipline: as to its *origin* a gift to us from God, as to its *exercise* a discipline to which we continuously subject ourselves.

(ii) Consider, furthermore, *the twofold implication with respect to this harmony of brotherly love.* Note the two expressions with which verses 22 and 23 begin. If the grammatical uniformity of the Greek were retained, they would read, "HAVING PURIFIED YOUR SOULS . . . HAVING BEEN BORN ANEW." Both are participles in the present tense, indicating an act already completed, the effects of which continue into the present.

Are the two events one and the same in Peter's mind or are they to be distinguished? Is the cleansing to which he here refers the washing away of sin's guilt which obviously occurs in connection with one's reception of the new life in Christ, or does Peter have in mind some deeper purging that has taken place in the experience of these Christians, the continuing effect of which is to make them sensitive to, and intolerant of, the subtle evils that plague and poison the harmony of the Christian brotherhood?

Some expositors favour the first view, some the second. Professor Kenneth Wuest, for example, sees numerous indications that many of these believers had passed through a stage of spiritual decline and defeat in which they had "feigned" love for certain brethren when in fact their hearts were cold, when, as in the case of the Corinthian church, envies and bickerings had torn the fabric of their unity in Christ. "But," says Wuest, "when they started to obey the Word again, their souls were purified, and they came to have that fondness and affection for their Christian brethren which is the normal condition among saints who are living in obedience to God's Word."

What seems clear is that sincere, steadfast brotherly love implies two requisites: (a) *spiritual life* ("born anew"); and (b) *spiritual health* ("purified . . . souls").

Each of these, moreover, rests down upon a condition. The condition for cleansing is obedience: "HAVING PURIFIED YOUR SOULS BY YOUR OBEDIENCE TO THE TRUTH" (v. 22). The condition for the new birth is the entry, as of a seed falling into the ground, of the creative Word of God: "BORN ANEW, NOT OF PERISHABLE SEED, BUT OF IMPERISHABLE, THROUGH THE LIVING AND ABIDING WORD OF GOD" (v. 23).

If it be asked why Peter says nothing here about faith, the answer, it may be suggested, is that in both instances faith is essentially involved. Obedience to the truth, a condition of cleansing, is both an aspect and an attestation of faith—a living, continuing, submitting trust in the truth unveiled in the Gospel.

Alexander Maclaren used to insist that "faith in its depth is obedience". And he would add: "If our faith has any vitality in it, it carries in it the essence of all submission."

As for the new birth, "the living and abiding word of God" which brings it to pass, requires the hospitable soil of a trusting heart, else it is as seed lying fruitless on caked or stony ground.

The quotation from Isaiah 40: 6–8, used by Peter in verse 24, throws up the contrast between the perishability of all things mortal and the imperishable authority and vitality of what God utters.

And—to get back to the real thrust of this whole passage— one of his utterances, by the lips of His Son, is, "A new commandment I give to you, that you love one another" (John 13: 34).

Quoting is not enough. Being sentimental about it is not enough. *Act* on it. If the life and health of God are in you, you will.

2. But this healthy Christian harmony has *enemies*. Therefore the maintenance of this health becomes Peter's concern as he concludes the appeal for concord in the community of believers.

How is *physical* health maintained? By avoiding what is harmful and assimilating what is useful. It is not otherwise with the soul's health. "SO PUT AWAY ALL MALICE AND ALL GUILE AND INSINCERITY AND ENVY AND ALL SLANDER. LIKE NEWBORN BABES, LONG FOR THE PURE SPIRITUAL MILK, THAT BY IT YOU MAY GROW UP TO SALVATION; FOR YOU HAVE TASTED THE KINDNESS OF THE LORD" (2: 1–3).

"Put away" is another of Peter's aorist imperatives: "Once for all renounce, have done with . . . !" Does this mean that provocations and temptations to these brotherhood-destroying evils will never reach us? Not at all. Not any more than having good health means that germs never invade our bodies. Doctors will tell us that germs of one sort or another are always there, threatening our health. The point is that so long as the health-tone of the body is up to normal, the resistance to germs is sufficiently strong to repel their attack and forestall the infection they would produce.

Here are five mischievous germs to repel, says Peter:

"MALICE" heads the list. It does so perhaps because the

apostle wants us to think of the four mischievous things that follow as forms or varieties of malice. In this case malice is the badness of ill-will which was so prevalent throughout the pagan world of early Christian times. Even non-Christian philosophers could not ignore it.

"GUILE" comes next. It is the evil of trickiness and craftiness. It is a first-cousin to—

"INSINCERITY" (which the *New English Bible* calls "pretence"). Actually, the Greek word is the one from which we derive "hypocrisy" and "hypocrites". It means literally to "speak under". It came to be used for the part played by actors on a stage who did their speaking from under the mask of whatever disguise was necessary or appropriate to the part they were taking. Under a hundred cloaks and in a hundred circumstances, it is the sin of Ananias and Sapphira. Whether it is a candidate for church membership giving answers that are poisoned by false motives or a preacher in the pulpit speaking dishonesties to his people, it is a cancelling out of reality that kills personal growth and torpedoes group confidence.

"ENVY" is the next of these mischief-makers. "I have read Hebrew, Greek, and Chaldee authors," said Marcus Aurelius, "but I have not found a cure for envy." This irritable and resenting discontent with another's superiority or another's fame or another's achievement—what a mean and unholy thing it is! One woman, when seeking Christ's cure, called her jealousy a "mental cancer".

And, finally, there is "SLANDER", for which the *New English Bible* employs the word "recrimination". It is the undisciplined tongue set going for any purpose whose objective is the disparagement of another person. It may be calculated slander. It may be the trivia of racy gossip. As James Moffatt points out: "Christians might be guilty of slander as well as exposed to it."

These—each and all—are the enemies of the soul's health. Of these—each and all—we are to be stripped. Peter's directive is at once drastic and decisive: "Put away . . . !"

In an hour of quiet group-sharing one person arose and said, "I tried too hard to prove that I was not too old, so I became peevish and fretful and tense. I sinned against the Holy Spirit ... I've let go my tension." The inner demon of insincerity and unreality had to be cornered, and, by the grace and power of the Holy Spirit, cast out.

So health comes—and stays.

So harmony comes—and abides.

III

BEHAVIOUR THAT WINS THROUGH
(PART I)

III

BEHAVIOUR THAT WINS THROUGH
(PART I)

"T HE world," wrote Alexander Maclaren, "takes its notions of God, most of all, from the people who say that they belong to God's family. They read us a great deal more than they read the Bible. They *see* us; they only *hear* about Jesus Christ."[1]

How right he was!

But Peter, long centuries earlier, was saying the same thing. *What* he says and *how* he says it must now have our attention as we turn to a new cycle of exhortations which he sends along to these troubled, hard-beset souls to whom he is writing.

II. APPEALS LINKED WITH THE PRACTICES OF THE PEOPLE OF GOD: 2:11—4:6

In language that is at once affectionate and solicitous Peter writes: "BELOVED, I BESEECH YOU AS ALIENS AND EXILES TO ABSTAIN FROM THE PASSIONS OF THE FLESH THAT WAGE WAR AGAINST YOUR SOUL. MAINTAIN GOOD CONDUCT AMONG THE GENTILES, SO THAT IN CASE THEY SPEAK AGAINST YOU AS WRONGDOERS, THEY MAY SEE YOUR GOOD DEEDS AND GLORIFY GOD ON THE DAY OF VISITATION" (vv. 11, 12).

A. Here, then, it is our behaviour as *pilgrims* that lies at the centre of the apostle's concern. The Greek words translated (in RSV) "aliens and exiles" are very similar in meaning, the former in all probability carrying overtones of historical

[1] Alexander Maclaren, *Expositions of the Holy Scriptures*, vol. XVI A (Eerdmans Publishing Company, Grand Rapids), p. 105.

circumstance as regards the groups of believers addressed, such as their being deprived of legal status, while the word for "exiles" speaks of the temporariness of their residence in whatever country they may be found.

Those who have fondness for the origin and history of words will note with interest that the word for "aliens" is the Greek *paroikous*, from which is derived the familiar ecclesiastical term *parish*. Originally a "parish" was a community of Christian believers distinguished by the fact that their real home was not of earth but of heaven, their real citizenship was not within empire, republic, or monarchy, but within the kingdom of God. Many an ancient churchman likened the Christian Church to Israel's captivity in Babylon. What would those churchmen think of the typical "parish" in America where to so great a degree the Church has made itself at home in Babylon, more influenced by, than influencing, it?

It is to the pilgrim Church that Peter addresses himself in a twofold summons:

1. He first calls for a *discipline that is inward and private:* "ABSTAIN FROM THE PASSIONS OF THE FLESH THAT WAGE WAR AGAINST YOUR SOUL." I have no difficulty in agreeing with Cranfield that "flesh" is here used in its "Pauline sense", which means that it is not necessarily a reference to sex or sexuality, and it is not necessarily to be identified with some vague thing called our "lower nature", with an implied slander against the bodily instincts. This whole manner of speaking is neither true to the revelation that comes to us through Hebrew thought nor the revelation that reaches us through the New Testament. How right is Jowett when he observes that, in Peter's vocabulary, "lusts" includes "not only the carnal desire, but the jealous eye and the itching palm!"[1]

In Galatians 5 : 19–21 Paul puts fifteen evils in the category of "works of the flesh". At least two-thirds of them have no

[1] J. H. Jowett, *The Redeemed Family of God* (Hodder and Stoughton Limited, London), p. 80.

connection with what is popularly called "fleshliness" or
passion. Of course, "drunkenness" is an enemy of the soul.
But so is "anger". So is "jealousy". So is "party-spirit"—
and its twin, "dissension". Indeed the basic evil of self-assertiveness, for which Christ's treatment is crucifixion, will be
forever trying to regain a foothold. The holy discipline of
watchfulness is the price of winning in the war against all that
wars against the soul.

2. In verse 12 Peter calls for an *outward and public deport-
ment* that is the convincing reflection of the inner discipline:
"MAINTAIN GOOD CONDUCT AMONG THE GENTILES, SO THAT IN
CASE THEY SPEAK AGAINST YOU AS WRONGDOERS, THEY MAY
SEE YOUR GOOD DEEDS AND GLORIFY GOD ON THE DAY OF
VISITATION." In effect Peter is saying two things here:

(*a*) As Christians, let fine behaviour be your *vocation*. "Maintain" it, keep it up, with no wearying and no vacillation. The
expression "having your conversation honest" in the Authorized Version, in the light of today's usage of both of these
words, is totally inadequate. The word for "conversation"
embraces all of our visible behaviour, while the word for
"honest" comes much closer to meaning "beautiful". As
Selwyn points out, the richness of the adjective seems to say
that the conduct in question "is not only good, but *appears*
so". There is a becomingness about it that is handsome.

(*b*) As Christians, let fine behaviour be your *vindication*. To
give high impulse to fine conduct Peter supplies a high motivation: "SO THAT IN CASE THEY SPEAK AGAINST YOU AS WRONG-
DOERS, THEY MAY SEE YOUR GOOD DEEDS AND GLORIFY GOD ON
THE DAY OF VISITATION" (v. 12). The Christians of the first
century were accused of everything from cannibalism to subversion: cannibalism because of a twist given by the non-
Christians to the words "This is my body" in the Communion
Service, and subversion because of their refusal to give worship
to Caesar. But with the passing of time came correction and
vindication. Barclay quotes a pertinent paragraph from the
fourth-century historian Eusebius, who wrote:

"*At the same time* (as the Church was spreading from nation to nation) *the slandering accusations which had been brought against the whole Church also vanished, and there remained our teaching alone, which has prevailed over all, and which is acknowledged to be superior to all in dignity and temperance, and in divine and philosophical doctrines. So that none of them now dares to affix a base calumny upon our faith, or any such slander as our ancient enemies formerly delighted to utter.*"[1]

Eusebius may be charged with some measure of optimistic exaggeration, but his main contention is supportable: by the quality of their lives the early Christians *lived down* the vilest of the slanders that were hurled against them. And many a pagan, won over from persecution to identification, was made to give glory to God.

As for the phrase "on the day of visitation", its Old Testament overtones speak of judgment, although mercy and blessing are not excluded. On the other hand, it may be said, as Wuest does categorically, that in the New Testament wherever the word is used as "visit" or "visitation" it refers to God's mercy and grace. Other expositors are not so bold as to say this, some of them preferring the view that here the phrase points forward to the Day of Judgment.

B. Our behaviour as *citizens* comes up for consideration in verses 13–17 of chapter 2. If from the higher point of view of our heavenly citizenship it must be said that Christians are pilgrims on the earth (v. 11), from the lower point of view of the pilgrimage itself it must be said that Christians are earth-dwellers with actual citizenship responsibilities.

Therefore, says Peter, "BE SUBJECT FOR THE LORD'S SAKE TO EVERY HUMAN INSTITUTION, WHETHER IT BE THE EMPEROR AS SUPREME, OR TO GOVERNORS AS SENT BY HIM TO PUNISH THOSE WHO DO WRONG AND TO PRAISE THOSE WHO DO RIGHT" (vv. 13, 14).

"Be subject!" Getting hold of the meaning here is important. It is the controlling phrase for this section of the epistle.

[1] Eusebius, *The Ecclesiastical History*, 4.7.15.

The *New English Bible* renders it: "Submit yourselves." Although it has its limits, as we shall see, submission is fundamentally the Christian answer, in the civil order, to that anarchic self-assertiveness which is the mark of man in his fallen state.

Four things about this Christian posture of submission must be noted:

1. There is the *command* that requires it. The verb is an aorist imperative, as though Peter were saying, "Settle it once for all that this is to be the course of action for you to follow." While "human institution" is the translation both of the RSV and NEB and "ordinance of man" is the rendering of the AV, it is probably closer to Peter's real meaning to say "every divine institution among men". That is to say, the essential structures of society—government, trade, the family—are by God's appointment for man's well-being.

God is a God of order. Order is concerned with men in community. The ordered life of men in community demands, as an underlying principle, the voluntary subordination of individual interests to the maintenance of the order. This recognition is essential, says Peter. The Creator requires it.

2. There is the *compulsion* that governs this posture of submission. As a citizen the Christian lives under two controlling incentives that are not operative in the case of the non-Christian. They are revealed in the phrases "FOR THE LORD'S SAKE" (v. 13) and "IT IS GOD'S WILL" (v. 15). The first phrase may be taken to mean *for the sake of the One who Himself gave obedience to the state, showed proper respect for Pilate as governor, and commanded His followers to "render unto Caesar the things that are Caesar's"*. Or, somewhat negatively it may be construed to mean *so as not to bring dishonour on the name of Christ by unlawful conduct*.

An understanding of the second phrase requires us to have the whole of verse 15 in view: "FOR IT IS GOD'S WILL THAT BY DOING RIGHT (in submission to the authority of civil government) YOU SHOULD PUT TO SILENCE THE IGNORANCE OF FOOLISH

MEN." There were loose talkers who ran down the Christians
and slandered the Christian movement without knowledge or
reason. It is God's will, says Peter, that you Christians, by
your voluntary subjection to civil authority, your generally
law-abiding behaviour, shall silence the mouths (literally,
"muzzle") of those who are obstinately inclined to be fault-
finders. Whether the muzzling keeps them from talking or
shuts them up after they have started is not made clear from
the construction of Peter's words. The former meaning need
not be excluded, according to Selwyn, from whom we have
this whimsical comment: "it is better to prevent an ass from
braying than stop it when it has brayed."

It remains to be added that *submission* is not of necessity the
same as *obedience*. Peter knew well the difference between the
two. After the healing of the lame man at the Beautiful Gate,
He and John were told by the authorities, "speak no more
to any one in this name" (Acts 4: 17). But they did! For their
disobedience they were arrested and jailed. But to this they
offered no resistance. *They submitted.* Their sole defence was:
"We must obey God rather than man" (Acts 5: 29).

3. There are the *characteristics* that distinguish this posture
of submission. The first is freedom: "LIVE AS FREE MEN, YET
WITHOUT USING YOUR FREEDOM AS A PRETEXT FOR EVIL" (v. 16).
"Not, however, as though your freedom were there to provide
a screen for wrongdoing," is the much more vivid rendering
of the *New English Bible*. That is to say, Christ has given you
the true freedom, which is freedom from sin, but do not fancy
that in your emancipated state you have a right to jettison
your citizenship duties, thus bringing your professed spiritual
freedom into ill repute.

That much is clear. What is less obvious but highly significant is the overtone carried by the clause "live as free men".
Selwyn points out that, whether "men" be understood as
referring only to Christian men or to men in general, the underlying idea requires us to place Peter on the side of a "liberal
as distinguished from an absolutist or totalitarian conception

of the State". He goes on to say that "... the idea that men are free of totalitarian political philosophy, and accounts for such modern attempts to suppress Christianity by various forms of persecution as we have seen in Russia and Germany".[1]

The other characteristic of Christian submission is *fidelity*: "LIVE AS SERVANTS OF GOD" (v. 16). In being subordinate to the State, Christians are not giving their ultimate loyalty to Caesar, but to God. In all faithfulness they are the slaves of God, whose "service", as the Prayer Book has it, is "perfect freedom".

4. Finally, there are the *categories* in which this posture of submission exhibits itself: "HONOUR ALL MEN. LOVE THE BROTHERHOOD. FEAR GOD. HONOUR THE EMPEROR" (v. 17).

It is not unreasonable, I think, to take these, not as four equally independent clauses, but as two couplets of clauses, with a somewhat closer relationship between the clauses in each bracket.

Worked out, it would read, Show that you value all men, but within the Christian fellowship let the love which Christ imparts inspire amongst you its own peculiar intimacy.

All men are recipients of the creature-life God bestows, all men are within the compass of the death that Christ dies; therefore, no matter how vain or vicious they may be, esteem them (which is a different thing from *admiring* them) and never exploit them.

As for your colleagues in Christ, it is fitting that the honour you give to men universally should deepen into that profound attachment and goodwill by which you are bound to those who share your faith in Jesus Christ.

I have a beloved friend in Christ who says, "When love gets low, criticism gets high. I find in myself, whenever I get out of touch with Christ, I begin to be critical of others. But when I am in living touch with Christ and therefore filled with love, then that love hides a multitude of sins."

"LOVE THE BROTHERHOOD!" "Brotherhood" is Peter's word for the "Church". He is the only New Testament writer who

---

[1] *Op. cit.*, p. 174.

uses it. He seems to prefer it to "Church", a word that appears nowhere in his letter. "Brotherhood" makes the Church, as someone has remarked, "an extension of the family".

The second couplet might be drawn out in paraphrase thus: Keep giving your reverence to God, but meanwhile continue to pay respect to the emperor.

This may be regarded as reminiscent of Proverbs 24: 21, "My son, fear the Lord and the king, and do not disobey either of them." It is noteworthy, however, that Peter will not use the same word for the recognition to be given each of them. The ruler is to be *esteemed* as symbolizing God's order of government, but God is to be held in *worshipful awe* as alone deserving of our supreme devotion.

Out of the later Diocletian persecutions of the Christians has come the story of Genesius, an actor who was playing a part in a burlesque on the rites and customs of the hated believers. In the midst of the play, as though the Holy Spirit suddenly shamed him for straying from the faith of the Christian home in which he was born, he cried out, "I want to receive the grace of Christ, that I may be born again, and be set free from the sins which have been my ruin!" The incredulous crowd saw the mock baptism that was being pantomimed turn in a trice into a hallowed moment of conversion as Genesius, fearlessly proclaiming his faith, cried out towards Diocletian: "Illustrious emperor, and all of you who have laughed loudly at this parody, believe me, Christ is the true king!"

Unmoved, save to fury, Diocletian ordered that he first be ripped with claws, then burned with torches, and finally beheaded. Before the end he was heard to cry: "There is no king except Christ, whom I have seen and whom I worship. For Him I will die a thousand times. I am sorry for my sin, and for becoming so late a soldier of the true King."[1]

"Illustrious emperor"? Yes. No vile epithet is flung at him. But Christ, Son of the everlasting Father, is King! A reverence

[1] H. B. Workman, *Persecution in the Early Church* (Epworth Press, Wyvern ed., London: 1960), pp. 126, 127 (Abingdon Press, Nashville, Tenn.).

for the Highest in heaven that forever transcends the highest on earth!

C. Peter moves now to a consideration of our Christian deportment as *servants*. The paragraph involved covers the remainder of the chapter.

Three centres of emphasis are easy to identify:

1. The first may be described as *a mandate that obligates*: "SERVANTS, BE SUBMISSIVE TO YOUR MASTERS WITH ALL RESPECT, NOT ONLY TO THE KIND AND GENTLE BUT ALSO TO THE OVERBEARING" (v. 18).

For "servants" we might as well read "slaves", for that is what they were. Since the Greek word is not the one ordinarily used for "slave" in the New Testament, but rather a term reserved more especially for domestic servants, Professor Wuest translates it "household slaves".

It is estimated that in the apostolic age the Roman Empire had not less than 60,000,000 slaves. It was a world made to measure for patricians and masters, who saw no point in working when there were these "chattels" who could do everything for them. While not all by far were chained to menial tasks— there were doctor-slaves, teacher-slaves, actor-slaves and so on—there was one thing that all had in common: they were devoid of rights. In this area of thought Aristotle's philosophy had come to full flower: "There can be no friendship nor justice toward inanimate things, indeed, not even towards a horse or an ox, nor yet towards a slave as a slave. For master and slave have nothing in common; a slave is a living tool, just as a tool is an inanimate slave."[1]

To be sure, not all masters took advantage of their powers of life and death over their slaves. Some were even fond of their servants, in that condescending way in which conscious superiors look down, benevolently bemused, on their hopeless inferiors!

At best, however, the slave's lot was one in which he was not a person but a thing. For him the most simple human rights

[1] Quoted by Barclay, *The Letters of James and Peter* (Westminster Press, Philadelphia: 1960), p. 250 (St. Andrew Press, Edinburgh).

did not exist. It is this sociological context within which we must view the duty that Peter lays on the slaves that were to be found in these harried congregations where soon his message would be read.

No New Testament writer, and not least Peter, makes any attack on the institution of human slavery. Nor does any writer incite the Christian slaves to mount an offensive against it. (Meanwhile, of course, the formidable mountain was being drilled and packed with the dynamite of the Gospel and the new attitude it brought with it, and one day the explosion would be touched off.)

It is neither as social philosopher nor as social reformer that Peter is here speaking. The issue to which he addresses himself is this: within the realities of the existing social situation how ought Christian slaves to deport themselves in relation to their masters? So addressing himself, the one point he scores is that slaves who claim Christ as Saviour and Lord must be prepared to suffer injustice and mistreatment without rancour or retaliation.

Go on giving what is expected of you, even though at times your master is tyrannical, oppressive, and cruel! In the circumstances you will by this means do more to advance the testimony of Christ and the influence of the Church than if you are rebellious, recalcitrant, and resentful.

This is your duty! Here is a mandate that obligates!

2. A second centre of emphasis in our passage may be described as *a motive that sublimates*: "FOR ONE IS APPROVED IF, MINDFUL OF GOD, HE ENDURES PAIN WHILE SUFFERING UNJUSTLY" (v.19).

Recall George Herbert's verses:

> "*A servant with this clause*
> *Makes drudgery divine:*
> *Who sweeps a room as for Thy laws*
> *Makes that and the action fine.*"[1]

[1] George Herbert, "The Elixir", published in *Seventeenth Century Prose and Poetry*, Robert P. T. Coffin and Alexander M. Witherspoon, editors (Harcourt, Brace and Company, New York: 1946), p. 121.

Where motive is pitched so high that its ultimate quest is the approval of *God* something happens to the drabbest job or the enduring of the meanest insult that gives it a touch of the sublime.

Think not, says Peter, that there is anything praiseworthy in your taking a lashing if you deserve it. It is said that offences for which slaves were most commonly beaten were pilfering and impudence. This might well be in Peter's mind—and theirs— as he cautions them against deriving any self-pitying compensation from such punishment. "FOR WHAT CREDIT IS IT, IF WHEN YOU DO WRONG AND ARE BEATEN FOR IT YOU TAKE IT PATIENTLY? BUT IF WHEN YOU DO RIGHT AND SUFFER FOR IT YOU TAKE IT PATIENTLY, YOU HAVE GOD'S APPROVAL" (v. 20).

This overplus of grace, giving a supernatural distinction to the discipleship of the Christian, echoes the words of Jesus: "For if you love those who love you, what reward have you? Do not even the tax collectors the same? And if you salute only your brethren, what more are you doing than others? Do not even the Gentiles do the same?" (Matthew 5: 46, 47).

3. And now, coming to one of the great moments in this epistle, we have a third centre of emphasis wherein we find *a model that illuminates*: "FOR TO THIS YOU HAVE BEEN CALLED BECAUSE CHRIST ALSO SUFFERED FOR YOU, LEAVING YOU AN EXAMPLE, THAT YOU SHOULD FOLLOW IN HIS STEPS" (v. 21).

As Peter lifts Him up, Jesus Christ is a pattern of suffering whom we are to view from two quite different standpoints:

(*a*) From one point of view He is a model that has *imitative* value. He has left us an "example" which we are to "follow". The Greek word for "example" signifies, says Beare, "the model of handwriting to be copied by the schoolboy". This, its literal meaning, passes easily into its figurative significance: a model of conduct intended for reproduction.

Just as it has been shown that God has "called" His people "out of darkness into his marvellous light" (2: 9), and just as it will later be shown that God has "called" them "to his

eternal glory" (5 : 10), so it is now shown by the apostle that
God *calls* His people to the patient bearing of a suffering which
they may have done nothing to deserve. In this suffering,
however, they are to remember—and by grace to reproduce—
the conduct of their Saviour, who, though He was without
shadow of blame, suffered beyond compare.

The example He set was that of *undeserved* suffering: "HE
COMMITTED NO SIN ; NO GUILE WAS FOUND ON HIS LIPS" (v. 22).

The example He set was that of *unembittered* suffering:
"WHEN HE WAS REVILED, HE DID NOT REVILE IN RETURN" (v.
23). (Both the prophetic language of Isaiah 53 and the historical language of Mark 15 : 17–20, 29–32 would seem to have
been present in Peter's mind.)

The example He set was that of *unretaliating* suffering:
"When he suffered, he did not threaten" (v. 23).

The example He set was that of *unfrustrated* suffering: "HE
TRUSTED TO HIM WHO JUDGES JUSTLY" (v. 23). (Literally, He
handed himself over. Just as Judas in betrayal "delivered up"
(same word) his Lord to the soldiers and the High Priest, just
as the Jews "delivered" him to Pilate, and just as Pilate
"delivered" Him to the soldiers for execution, so He at the last
"delivered" Himself with unshatterable confidence into the
keeping of the Father who judges with perfect equity.)

Can we point to any who have followed this example?

On a May day in 1555 Bishop Hugh Latimer, soon to burn
at the stake for his anti-papal, Reformed convictions, composed an open letter "To All Unfeigned Lovers of God's
Truth".

"Die once we must," he wrote ; *"how and where we know not
. . . Here is not our home: let us therefore accordingly consider
things, having always before our eyes that heavenly Jerusalem
and the way thereto in persecution. And let us consider all the dear
friends of God, how they have gone after the example of our Saviour
Jesus Christ; Whose footsteps let us also follow, even to the gallows
if God's will be so, not doubting but as He rose again the third day,
even so shall we do at the time appointed of God, that is, when the*

trump shall blow, and the angel shall shout, and the Son of Man shall appear."[1]

Later that year, when the dignity of Oxford town was demoted to that of a persecutor's den, they fed both Latimer and his friend Ridley to the devouring flames; but not until Latimer, astonishingly composed, said to his colleague in martyrdom, "Be of good comfort, Master Ridley, and play the man. We shall this day light such a candle by God's grace in England as I trust shall never be put out!"

That Man from Nazareth had not left His "example" in vain!

(*b*) There remains a second point of view from which we must, according to Peter, regard Jesus and His sufferings: "HE HIMSELF BORE OUR SINS IN HIS BODY ON THE TREE" (v. 24). Seen in this aspect of His Saviourhood, Jesus and His suffering provide us with a model that, far from having imitative value, has *incomparable* value.

It is as though Peter said, My Christian brothers, I would set before you the exemplary suffering of our Lord, in which we see His meekness and quiet fortitude under the strokes of injustice; but I must remind you that in His suffering He went far beyond the giving of an example that we are to emulate: He did something that no one else could ever have done, and in the doing of which He can never be imitated.

We must see this clearly. "A martyr may be an example of patient suffering; he cannot bear our sins." Here is atonement, unapproachable in its uniqueness.

In pointing this out I do not forget the reasonable caution of those expositors who emphasize the *practical* rather than the *doctrinal* motive by which our author is moved in this passage. There is danger, I freely admit, that we shall read into it, and especially into its particular terms, theological concepts that have been sharpened to a razor's edge in the centuries since the New Testament was completed.

[1] Marcus L. Loane, *Masters of the English Reformation* (The Church Book Room Press, London: 1956), p. 129.

Fortunate Peter! He did not have to worry whether he would be accused of being a "disciple of Anselm" or a "follower of Abelard", whether he would be tagged a "supra-lapsarian Calvinist" or a "semi-Pelagian Arminian". Out of the rich overflow of his inspired heart he was free simply to set forth the *truth* in all of its staggering massiveness, mystery, and might.

Let us try now to distinguish four really great things in these two remaining verses of the chapter:

(*a*) The *great redemption by sacrifice:* "HE HIMSELF BORE OUR SINS IN HIS BODY ON THE TREE." The Old Testament is in full view here, as a mirror for reflecting the meaning of the Cross. The body of a criminal was left hanging on a tree until nightfall (Deuteronomy 21: 22, 23). The Passover Feast required a sacrificial lamb that was "without blemish" (Exodus 12: 5). On the Day of Atonement the high priest ritually transferred to the scapegoat "all the iniquities of the people of Israel, and all their transgressions, all their sins" (Leviticus 16: 21). Isaiah, portraying the Suffering Servant, sees Him as having "borne our griefs and carried our sorrows", sees Him as "wounded for our transgressions . . . bruised for our iniquities", sees Him as the One through whose "stripes we are healed" (Isaiah 53: 4, 5).

Some expositors have got themselves into needless difficulties by attempting to isolate one or another of these priestly and prophetic pictures, and then to make *all* that Peter says fit the picture exactly. Thus Professor Beare would dismiss any connection between Peter's thought and the scapegoat ritual on the ground that "the scapegoat was not slain in sacrifice, but driven away into the wilderness".[1]

More likely is the view that our apostle has woven together several strands of prophetic symbol and utterance from the Old Testament, and that what we see in the tapestry of truth thus produced is an act of God in Christ in which the shame, the alienation, the scandal, of our sin, as well as the judicial doom

[1] F. W. Beare, *The First Epistle of Peter.*

attached thereto, were caught up by Him, dealt with, and put away. Archbishop Leighton's words have a vividness worthy of Peter himself: "The sins of all, in all ages before and after, who were to be saved, all their guiltiness met together on His back upon the Cross."

The only fitting answer we can make to *that* is the cry, out of our dust and ashes:

> "*My faith would lay her hand*
> *On that meek head of Thine,*
> *While as a penitent I stand*
> *And here confess my sin.*"

The great redemption by sacrifice!

(*b*) As a consequence we have *the great release from sin*: "THAT WE MIGHT DIE TO SIN, AND LIVE TO RIGHTEOUSNESS" (v. 24). The teaching at this point is radical. We can be sure that Peter would never deny St. Paul's right to stress at times the *imputed* righteousness which is a proper part of justification by faith on the ground of atonement made. At the same time we must not dilute Peter's insistence that Christ's atonement, received in the full measure of its divine intention, results in something deeply, transformingly subjective, namely, our actual release from sin's guilt and grip, and our actual rehabilitation for a life of righteousness.

The phrase "that we might die to sin" may be literally, if awkwardly, translated, "having become off with respect to sins". Selwyn says it is best translated "having ceased from" or "having abandoned" sins. And this, it is made plain, with a view to *living in righteousness!*

Theologians have a five-guinea word known as "antinomianism". It's a clumsy thing, not at all precise. Literally, it means "against the law". Historically, it is applied to those in the Christian community who misunderstood or perverted the doctrine of grace. To St. Paul's question, "Shall we sin that grace may abound?" they would reply, "Yes. Why not? God accepted us in Christ apart from the law. And since to be in Christ is a non-forfeitable position, He will continue to accept us whether we sin or not."

Actually, I suppose, there is very little of such blatant antinomianism in the Church today. But I suggest that there is far too much of *tacit* antinomianism—not so much explicit as implicit. When a contemporary theologian says that "God can do nothing with sin but forgive it", and when the word is circulated that, as Sangster critically describes it, "there is something to be forgiven in the best deed of the best man on the best day of his life",[1] you have a mixture of half-truth and error that drains from the Gospel the power of character-cleansing and life-control in righteousness, of which men like Paul and Peter make so much.

Professor Harold DeWolf contends that the "existentialist" theologians of our day, including the most famous of all of them, Dr. Paul Tillich, move "on the very edge of antinomian-ism, that is, the repudiation of all moral law as related to salvation". He strikes particularly at Tillich's definition of justification as the "acceptance of acceptance"—our simple acceptance of God's acceptance of us as sinners—with no serious stress on repentance of spirit or sanctification of life. This, says DeWolf, "tends to lessen the moral earnestness of Christian faith".[2]

Evangelicals are prepared to applaud such a criticism as this. Are they equally prepared to face up to the implications of it for their view of sin and grace? Do they realize that in the atonement of Christ God's burden is not only how He can *call* sinners righteous, but how He can *make* them such.

(c) The great release from sin is amplified, in Peter's thought, by reference to *the great restoration to soundness*: "BY HIS WOUNDS YOU HAVE BEEN HEALED" (v. 24).

"You!" A sudden shift from "we" in the preceeding sentence. It has been guessed that a majority of Peter's

[1] W. E. Sangster, *You Can Be A Saint* (Epworth Press, London: 1957), p. 10.

[2] Harald DeWolf, *Present Trends in Christian Thought* (Association Press, New York: 1960), pp. 73, 74.

readers would be slaves. They would grasp the meaning of his word "stripes". Actually, it is singular in the Greek; and the word, used nowhere else in the New Testament, means *weal*: the huge welt raised on the back of the slave who is given the lash.

Yes, they would know what it meant, in *physical* torture at any rate, for Jesus to be subjected to a Roman scourging. So Peter, fully aware of the fitness of his quotation, borrows from Isaiah (53 : 5) and assures them that by Christ's wounding the sin-diseased souls of men are healed. The paradox is well caught in an exclamation by Theodoret: "A new and strange method of healing; the doctor suffered the cost, and the sick received the healing!"[1]

> *"By Thine agonizing pain*
> *And sweat of blood, we pray,*
> *By Thy dying love to man,*
> *Take all our sins away:*
> *Burst our bonds and set us free;*
> *From all iniquity release;*
> *O remember Calvary,*
> *And bid us go in peace."*[2]

(*d*) Finally, through the incomparable sufferings of Christ we have *the great return to safety*: "FOR YOU WERE STRAYING LIKE SHEEP, BUT HAVE NOW RETURNED TO THE SHEPHERD AND GUARDIAN OF YOUR SOULS" (v. 25).

The *New English Bible*, in its reading "now you have turned towards the Shepherd and Guardian of your souls", is disappointingly weak. The prodigal was still in the "far country" when he "turned *towards*" the father's house. Peter's thought is much stronger than that. To continue the analogy with the familiar parable, the picture here is not that of the son *on the way* home, but that of the son *at* home—welcomed, received, reinstated, rejoicing.

[1] Quoted by Selwyn, *Ibid.*, p. 181.
[2] Charles Wesley, *The Methodist Hymn Book*.

Our apostle's metaphor, however, is different. Undoubtedly
it rises out of his knowledge of many a passage in the Old
Testament, together with some of the choicest sayings of His
Lord. The background afforded by Isaiah 53 seems particularly
prominent. When Moffatt makes Peter say, "For you were
astray like lost sheep", the echo from Isaiah 53: 6 is clear,
"All we like sheep have gone astray; we have turned every one
to his own way; and the Lord has laid on him the iniquity of us
all."

And when Peter says, You have now "returned to the
Shepherd and Guardian of your souls", the echo of Luke 15: 3
is tenderly resonant, "What man of you, having a hundred
sheep, if he has lost one of them, does not leave the ninety-
nine in the wilderness, and go after the one which is lost until
he finds it? And when he has found it, he lays it on his shoulder
rejoicing. And when he comes home, he calls together his friends
and his neighbours, saying to them, 'Rejoice with me, for I
have found my sheep which was lost'."

Excellent! But now a question: whose concern is it chiefly
to watch over the spiritual well-being and safety of these
returned wanderers? Peter's answer: the One who is called
"Shepherd" and "Guardian".

The latter word is the one in Greek from which we derive
bishop, the *episcopos*, easily recognizable in our familiar
adjective *episcopal*. Peter's use of it in this context tells us
nothing about its present ecclesiastical meaning. Farthest
removed from his mind was the thought of any Pope or Prelate
or Primate who might be held officially accountable for the
care of souls. It is the oversight and care of the supreme
Pastor, our Lord Himself, that the apostle would extol.

As Shepherd, He offers provision; as Guardian, He offers
protection.

Thus Peter's keen ears catch the affectionate accents of the
Shepherd's voice:

> *My sheep . . .*
> *I gave my life for them . . .*

They hear my voice . . .
They follow me . . .
I give them eternal life . . .
And they shall never perish . . .
And no one shall snatch them out of my hand

Peter! Bless you!

What treasures you have unveiled to us while talking about such homely matters as how the household slaves shall behave before their masters!

D. The next appeal, which moves us into chapter 3, is directed to WIVES AND HUSBANDS (3: 1–7).

Each set of spouses is addressed in the same manner: "Likewise you wives" (v. 1) . . . "Likewise you husbands" (v. 7). The "likewise" is probably best understood as referring back to this principle of *submission* which was introduced in 2: 13.

Before Peter's instructions are examined—and the wives might as well know in advance that he has about six times as much to say to them as he does to their husbands!—we must be made aware of several background facts. Peter is not about to discourse on the status of male and female. His aim is much narrower. His intention is severely practical—though much that he says suggests principles that are broadly applicable to the successful management of the husband-wife relationship in any culture.

The concrete situation he has before him is one in which many—perhaps a strong majority—of the wives addressed are Christians with pagan husbands. It is presumed, on the other hand, that the husbands who will read this letter are Christians with Christian wives. Christian husbands of the first century, even if their wives declined for a while to follow them in the faith, faced nothing like the acute problems, complications, and hardships of believing wives with unbelieving husbands. We need to bear in mind that this is the historical context within which Peter's directives are given.

What, then, is the behaviour for which he calls?

1. Consider the duties of Christian *wives*:

(*a*) There is *respectfulness, and its intention*: "BE SUBMISSIVE TO YOUR HUSBANDS, SO THAT SOME, THOUGH THEY DO NOT OBEY THE WORD, MAY BE WON WITHOUT A WORD BY THE BEHAVIOUR OF THEIR WIVES" (v. 1). The NEB, I think, improves on this: "you women must accept that authority of your husbands, so that if there are any of them that disbelieve the Gospel they may be won over, without a word being said."

In God's order for the family the household must have a head. That head is the husband. The wife must respectfully recognize him as such. Even when he is far from deserving that respect, she must not be quick to forget his position.

If he is an unbeliever—even a defiant one—her attitude, her bearing, and her demeanour will go further towards winning him to Christ than back-talk, bad temper, or even pious-sounding pleadings and warnings. A passage from Augustine's *Confessions* is touchingly to the point. Of his mother Monica he says:

> "*When she came to marriageable age, she was bestowed upon a husband and served him as her Lord, and she did all she could to win him to Thee, speaking to him of Thee by her deportment, whereby Thou madest her beautiful and reverently lovable and admirable to her husband. . . . Finally, when her husband was now at the very end of his earthly life she won him unto Thee.*"[1]

(*b*) There is *faithfulness, and its incentive*: "WHEN THEY SEE YOUR REVERENT AND CHASTE BEHAVIOUR" (v. 2). The translators of the RSV have elected to take the Greek phrase "in fear" and render it "reverent". What your husbands should see in you, says Peter, is *your chaste behaviour in fear*. Such, at any rate, would be a literal rendering. Never let any occasion arise wherein your husband has reason to suspect your fidelity to him and to your marital obligations. And your incentive for giving him this loyalty is that you hold God in such high and reverent regard.

[1] Saint Augustine, *Confessions*, IX., 19, 22.

(c) There is *modesty, and its inwardness*: "LET NOT YOURS BE THE OUTWARD ADORNING WITH BRAIDING OF HAIR, DECORATION OF GOLD, AND WEARING OF ROBES, BUT LET IT BE THE HIDDEN PERSON OF THE HEART WITH IMPERISHABLE JEWEL OF A GENTLE AND QUIET SPIRIT" (v. 3). We misread these words if we think of them as constituting simply a *ban* on braiding hair, or using gold, or wearing a robe. Rhetorically it is the same kind of "Hebraism" that we find in John 6: 27, "Do not labour for the food which perishes, but for the food which endures to eternal life." Obviously our Lord does not prohibit daily work for daily bread. What He does condemn is an inverted sense of values in which food for the body is reckoned to be more important than the life of the soul.

Similarly, Peter is asking wives to observe the duty of modesty—the word means far more than primness or prudery; it means attractive self-restraint—in the realization that, after all, what makes a wife desirable to her husband is not something as external as her coiffure but something as internal as her character. This beauty cannot be hung around the neck like a flashing pendant. It grows within like a lovely flower. Even if some coarse and callous husband fails to appreciate it, it is "in God's sight . . . very precious" (v. 4).

This modesty *in the grain*, so to speak, was exemplified by the noble women among God's chosen of the past, notably by Abraham's wife, Sarah. "Sarah obeyed Abraham, calling him lord" (v. 6).

Since "obeyed" is in the aorist tense, it is taken in either of two ways: (1) as referring to Sarah's habitual deference to Abraham viewed panoramically, as one single act, or (2) as pointing to the time when it was revealed to Abraham that they were to have a son, notwithstanding their advanced age. If the latter, then the relevant verse must be read in the AV: "After I am waxed old shall I have pleasure, *my lord* being old also?" (Genesis 18: 12). Astonished and sceptical though she was, she nevertheless bowed to his authority.

And you Christian wives, says Peter, "are now her children

(spiritually her descendants) if you do right and let nothing terrify you" (v. 6), such as the unkind or abusive treatment of your husbands. If "you do not give way to hysterical fears", is the way Phillips renders it.

2. Consider the duties of Christian *husbands*:

That sigh you hear is from the wives, impatiently saying, "Well, it's about time!"

"LIKEWISE YOU HUSBANDS, LIVE CONSIDERATELY WITH YOUR WIVES, BESTOWING HONOUR ON THE WOMAN AS THE WEAKER SEX, SINCE YOU ARE JOINT HEIRS OF THE GRACE OF LIFE, IN ORDER THAT YOUR PRAYERS MAY NOT BE HINDERED" (v. 7).

(*a*) To start with, a Christian husband owes his wife a *considerateness that never forgets its obligation*: "LIVE CONSIDERATELY WITH YOUR WIVES" is a simple and, very probably, fair rendering of a Greek clause that admits of much discussion. The AV, "dwell with them according to knowledge", comes much closer to the original. The Greek participle for "dwelling with" in some contexts has reference to sexual congress, though most expositors feel that this meaning is not in Peter's mind. If, however, this facet of meaning is to be seen here, the force of the apostle's directive is clear: Husbands, the sexual aspect of your marriage, far from being denied or despised (as it was in fact by an early sect called the Encratites), must be observed with an understanding ("Knowledge") of the mutual interests involved.[1]

If this meaning is ruled out, then the duty enjoined is that of an over-all thoughtfulness and respect, such as would never be accorded to a wife in a culture in which she was regarded as a thing, not a person; as a chattel to be owned, not a partner to be loved.

(*b*) Furthermore, and as something closely related, the Christian husband *owes his wife a courtesy that never forgets her needs*: "BESTOWING HONOUR ON THE WOMAN AS THE WEAKER SEX" (v. 7). Neither the noun "vessel" (as it is in the original)

[1] Cf. Selwyn, *Ibid.* pp. 186, 187.

nor the adjective "weaker" is intended to be derogatory. The whole New Testament, far from encouraging the then prevalent notion of woman's essential inferiority to man, strikes hard at it. The differences between the two are differences of function rather than of status. Peter's specific point is that a disparity of physical strength between husband and wife, such as normally is found, calls for a chivalrous attitude on his part.

(c) Still further, the Christian husband *owes his wife a comprehension that never forgets her spiritual equality with him*: "YOU ARE JOINT HEIRS OF THE GRACE OF LIFE" (v. 7). Even if she is not a believer, she is as surely included in the embrace of God's redeeming love in Christ as he is. If she is a Christian, then no matter how inferior Roman law may make her, she is as Bigg puts it, "his equal, and maybe his superior, in the eyes of God".[1]

Can it be imagined that where this decisive insight governs a man's Christian conduct he will take advantage of his wife, exploiting her submissiveness or demeaning her personality?

(d) Finally, the Christian husband *owes his wife a conscience that never forgets the danger of broken communion with God*: "THAT YOUR PRAYERS MAY NOT BE HINDERED" (v. 7). Some Greek authorities feel that "your" applies only to the husband, others that it may be taken as a reference to both husband and wife. The technicality is not important. The truth at stake does in fact apply to both.

Indeed to stress this point is an excellent way to summarize all that Peter has been saying about the Christian behaviour of those who are married partners. Throughout the passage he is talking about *responsibilities*, not about *rights*. When these responsibilities are mutually assumed and carried forward, there is almost never any need for worry or words over rights. Of one's years of pastoral experience in a downtown church, where much counselling was called for outside the bounds of one's congregation, I can testify that no marriage is secure when both spouses are obsessed with their so-called "rights".

[1] Bigg, *Ibid.*, p. 155.

Stability, serenity, and growing richness come when each is primarily concerned that *duties* are affectionately and generously discharged.

Even marriage at its best is not, from the Christian point of view, an end in itself. It is intended to serve a more ultimate end, namely, the fellowship of both partners with the God of love and grace, that so *His* glory may be realized. Selfishness on the part of either spouse will do more than cut their human communion : it will break into their life of prayer together, paralysing its freedom, draining off its sweetness.

The relevance of all this for Christian parents today could scarcely be more urgent than it is. Social workers are finding that generally "problem children" are the products of husbands and wives who are themselves problems—problems to one another. Divided, quarrelling, demanding husbands and wives are turning loose upon society a spate of neurotic children. Boys and girls who have seen no consistently maintained example of mutual affection and Christ-like self-discipline in the lives of their parents are not likely to mature into persons of balance, useful alike to the world and to the Kingdom of God.

This is not to say that one looks for Utopia even in a Christian home. "A Christian home," says Dr. Samuel Shoemaker, writing on "The Holy Spirit and Ourselves", "is not one in which the relationships are perfect . . . but one in which the imperfections and failures are acknowledged and where problems are worked out in prayer and obedience to the light God sends. In such homes there is great freedom for people to say what they think and express what they feel. There is not the repression of law imposed by one or both of the parents on the children, nor by somebody's temper or tears on everybody. People are allowed to grow up, to make mistakes, to be themselves, to laugh, to live through difficult crises or periods with privacy if they want it, with help if they want that."[1]

[1] Samuel M. Shoemaker, *With the Holy Spirit and With Fire* (Harper and Brothers, New York : 1960), p. 121.

This is being written in such a home, a quiet, lovely place in the rolling countryside of Hertfordshire, England. Four grown sons and a daughter—one son married and, the proud father of a little girl, beginning with his wife the happy team-work of prayer-guided parenthood which he first saw in his own father and mother—all five looking toward some phase or another of Christian service, all displaying the courtesy toward one another and the zestful interest in each other's activities which the observer recognizes as the sign of an emotionally healthy home life! I cannot imagine such children, forming such a network of happy relationships, coming from a home in which the husband and wife had ignored the plain duties so clearly brought forward by Peter in this section of our letter.

No, it isn't the millennium.

Neither is it the mess that, God knows, is fouling American and English social life today.

So, cast them in whatever role you will—pilgrims, citizens, servants, spouses—Christians are under bonds to Jesus Christ, and this loyalty soaks and stains their conduct wherever you find them. If it does not give them an all-inclusive *code* (which it doesn't), it gives them an all-important *cue* (which is greater).

IV

BEHAVIOUR THAT WINS THROUGH
(PART II)

BEHAVIOUR THAT WINS THROUGH
(PART II)

M Y host, in a home where I was staying, was reading his morning mail. Suddenly he began chuckling. The friend whose letter he was reading had concluded with these words: "I think of you, Donald, as a sane and practical Christian, not like those people who are so heavenly minded that they are no earthly use, and won't pay their rent!"

Peter, too, would have smiled. But beneath the smile would have been a sadness. Someone had failed—someone calling himself a Christian. Someone had ignored the smart and sting of Emerson's query, "How can I hear what you *say* when what you *are* is thundering in my ears?" Someone had scrambled the Christian logic of faith and works: the heavenly mind of belief must be poured into the earthly mould of behaviour.

Never will Peter allow the readers of his letter to get away from this. His interest, as we have seen, is not, in the main, theological but practical. For its thrust, however, it depends chiefly on the vehicle of exhortation, of counsel, of directive. We have chosen to use the word "appeals".

We return to these appeals as we find them in the second cycle: *appeals that are linked with the practices of the people of God*, commencing with chapter 2, verse 11, and proceeding through chapter 4, verse 6. Under review thus far has been our behaviour as *pilgrims*, as *citizens*, as *servants*, and as *married partners*. In the subdivision that now comes before us our attention is turned to the manner in which we are to deport ourselves in those circumstances of trouble which, in the case of Peter's readers, have begun to harass them and are due to grow worse rather than better.

Thus, to continue our outline, we have:

E. Our behaviour as *sufferers*: 3: 8—4: 6.

1. For one thing, it must be *behaviour that is consistent with Christian integrity*. This, it seems to me, is the chief stress of verses 8–12, including the use Peter makes of the extended quotation from Psalm 34.

"Integrity" is a worthy word, especially when it is set within the context of the grace of God. For in this context we see not only the brother but the brotherhood of Christian faith invested with a gift of righteousness and with a sense of *wholeness*. The man becomes a man of *one piece* in Christ. He is not a fraction of a man; he is an *integer*. And the brotherhood is one fellowship—not fragmentized, but integrated.

(*a*) Observe the *pattern which this Christian integrity traces*: "FINALLY, ALL OF YOU HAVE UNITY OF SPIRIT, SYMPATHY, LOVE OF THE BRETHREN, A TENDER HEART AND A HUMBLE MIND" (v. 8).

The sentence is transitional. It faces both ways: toward what has gone before and what follows.

Here are five colours or strands woven into this excellent pattern:

Unity-mindedness. The more literal meaning is *a disposition to mind the same things*. St. Paul's word provides a helpful commentary: "For those who live according to the flesh set their minds on the things of the flesh, but those who live according to the Spirit, set their minds on the things of the Spirit" (Rom. 8: 5). It is the apostle's way of saying, Brothers, attend to the interests of Christ and His Kingdom, with common longing, common eagerness, common concern, and you will find that your hearts are one in Him.

Sympathy-mindedness. It is the capacity for *feeling alike* or *feeling together*. It is Christianized social imagination: the ability to put oneself in the other person's place and to be, in some real measure, emotionally identified.

"I myself become the wounded person!"

Brother-mindedness. To have "love of the brethren" means that in that love, which is Christ's own gift to us, we take peculiar delight in one another because we are fellow-members of the family of God.

Tender-mindedness. The Greek word has classical origins. It is derived from a word that means "the bowels", and is connected with an ancient notion that the visceral part of man was the seat of strong emotion, whether of love or of anger.

Witness St. Paul's directive to the Ephesians: "Be ye kind one to another, *tender-hearted*, forgiving one another" (4: 30). We Christians must *show* it in a day that is afflicted with what one of our literary editors has strikingly called "compassion exhaustion". A civilization that is being stalked by tragedy needs to be newly stocked with tenderness.

Humble-mindedness. Why, we may ask, the difference between the AV, "be courteous" (joined by Phillips), and the rendering given in the RSV, the NEB, and Moffatt? *The difference is in the Greek text, some manuscripts having a form of the word that means "friendly", others a form that means "humble-minded".* Translators who prefer the former employ "courteous" as a way of drawing out the thought of friendliness.

The supreme illustration of this spirit, and the action to which it leans, is found in our Lord, and the classical setting forth of it is by St. Paul to the Philippians: "Have this mind among yourselves, which you have in Christ Jesus, who, though he was in the form of God, did not count equality with God a thing to be grasped, but emptied himself, taking the form of a servant, being born in the likeness of men" (2: 5, 6).

> *"The kingdoms of the earth go by*
> *In purple and in gold;*
> *They rise, they flourish, and they die,*
> *And all their tale is told.*
> *One Kingdom only is Divine,*
> *One banner triumphs still,*

> *Its King a servant, and its sign*
> *A gibbet on a hill.*"[1]

Unity-mindedness, sympathy-mindedness, brotherhood-mindedness, tender-mindedness, humble-mindedness—this is the pattern we trace in that Christian integrity which is to be manifested by the believer as a person and by the people of God as a fellowship.

(b) *The pressure against which this integrity triumphs:* "DO NOT RETURN EVIL FOR EVIL OR REVILING FOR REVILING; BUT ON THE CONTRARY BLESS, FOR TO THIS YOU HAVE BEEN CALLED, THAT YOU OBTAIN A BLESSING" (v. 9). The words of Jesus come instantly to mind: "Blessed are you when men hate you, and when they exclude you and revile you, and cast out your name as evil, on account of the Son of Man! . . . Love your enemies, do good to those who hate you, bless those who curse you" (Luke 6: 22, 27, 28).

A friend tells of a woman who was being treated by doctors but without benefit. They were baffled. She was wasting away, unable to digest her food. They requested that a minister be consulted. They said to him, "There is something here that we cannot touch. See if you can find out what it is." What the pastor found was nothing physical, but it was cancerous just the same: a terrible resentment and hatred against another woman who had been soliciting and, in some degree, securing the attentions of her husband. In one bitter outburst she said, "I could tear her limb from limb." The answer to her problem, she discovered, was not drugs but Christ. She surrendered to Him not only her revengefulness but herself. Before long her personal physician found her in church on Sunday, full of forgiveness, and radiant.

Pressures! Of course there are pressures. Unprincipled people may rip our reputations to shreds. Cruel people may fling one hurt at us after another. Spiteful people may cast our names to the rubbish pile.

---

[1] G. F. Bradby, quoted by D. T. Niles in *The Preacher's Calling to be Servant* (Lutterworth Press, London), p. 47 (Harper & Bros., New York).

Still, love's inner braces hold! No return in kind! Instead, blessing for cursing, kindness for cruelty, mercy for meanness.

Here, you see, is the deep, inner integrity that can take assault without collapsing. The Master within him gives the Christian the mastery of the pressures that are upon him.

(c) *The pleasure which this integrity takes:* "HE THAT WOULD LOVE LIFE AND SEE GOOD DAYS, LET HIM KEEP HIS TONGUE FROM EVIL AND HIS LIPS FROM SPEAKING GUILE" (v. 10). Peter makes an interesting alteration in the quotation from Psalm 34: 12. He is not content to have it read, "he that desireth life", where the immediate context indicates that the longing is conceived in terms of physical existence and temporal prosperity. No, Peter makes it read, literally, "he that desires (or wills) to love life".

Quite the opposite is the boredom, the cynicism, of a disillusioned Swinburne:

> "*From too much love of living,*
> *From hope and fear set free,*
> *We thank with brief thanksgiving*
> *Whatever gods may be*
> *That no life lives for ever,*
> *That dead men rise up never;*
> *That even the weariest river*
> *Winds somewhere safe to sea.*"[1]

They who are themselves empty find life empty. They who are themselves chaotic find the world a hopeless riddle.

On the contrary, those who, through the reconciling Saviour, are linked with the Everlasting Righteousness, know full well that, all the sorry sum of evils notwithstanding, "the eyes of the Lord *are* upon the righteous" and "The face of the Lord *is* against those who do evil" (v. 12). The integrity God has planted within them answers to the integrity they know belongs ultimately to the universe. So for them life is good.

---

[1] Charles Swinburne, "The Garden of Proserpine", published in *Victorian and Later English Poets* (The American Book Company, New York: 1949).

This, in worthy definition, is the pleasure of living which neither trouble nor the threat of trouble can take from them.

2. Let this be said too about our behaviour in suffering: it must be *behaviour that is committed to Christ's sovereignty.* Beginning with verse 13 a connection is established between the realized lordship of Christ and the Christian's security in the midst of attack: "NOW WHO IS THERE TO HARM YOU IF YOU ARE ZEALOUS FOR WHAT IS RIGHT. BUT EVEN IF YOU DO SUFFER FOR RIGHTEOUSNESS' SAKE, YOU WILL BE BLESSED. HAVE NO FEAR OF THEM, NOR BE TROUBLED, BUT IN YOUR HEARTS REVERENCE CHRIST AS LORD" (vv. 13–15).

The last clause is an important key. Its importance is blunted by the weak translations of it that appear in the RSV, the NEB, and in Phillips. The RSV reads: "In your hearts reverence Christ as Lord." The link with Isaiah 8 : 13 is obvious; and here, happily, the RSV brings us closer to the very great and moving thing with which both passages confront us: *"But the Lord of hosts, him you shall regard as holy; let him be your fear, and let him be your dread."* (The word was spoken to Judah at a time when foreign invasion was threatening.)

Note the phrase, "Him you shall regard (that is, acknowledge) as holy." A further clue to what is really meant by Peter is found in a powerful passage in Ezekiel 20. Commencing with verse 39, there is first the irony of a word from the Lord God in which Israel is told, *"Go serve every one of you his idols, now and hereafter, if you will not listen to me; but my holy name you shall no more profane with your gifts and your idols."* Then follows the prophetic word, looking forward to repentance and recovery, anticipating the abandonment of idols and the bringing of an acceptable offering. Whereupon it will come to pass, says the Lord God, *"I will manifest my holiness among you in the sight of the nations"* (20: 39, 41).

What, then, does it mean to acknowledge God as holy? It means to be so open to that holiness that whatever contradicts it, rivals it, discredits it, must go—swept clean away as He, responding to this acknowledgment, gathers up His people into a cleansing fellowship with Himself and makes "manifest" His holiness to them.

Small wonder that Bishop Stephen Neil, in his *Christian Holiness*, confesses his disappointment at the "Pelagian"[1] fashion in which translators and commentators alike have dealt with I Peter 3 : 15. It is a meagre view of it indeed that sees, or seems to see, nothing but a piece of counsel having to do with a well-cultivated reverence for Jesus Christ. Actually there are two things about it that are remarkable and enormously humbling. One is the authority Peter exercises in identifying "Christ" as the "Lord of Hosts" in the Isaiah source he quotes. Utterly unthinkable for a Jew to do unless he were convinced that Jesus Christ is in fact "very God of very God", not less than "very man of very man"! The other is the high demand that he makes upon his Christian friends to "sanctify in your hearts Christ as Lord", which is the rendering of the English Revised Version, and it is the best.

It is the apostle's way of saying, You have confessed Him as your Saviour. Now face up to the implications of His *lordship*. Let Him establish that lordship as real and unrivalled. Let Him catch you up into Himself so that the gracious, penetrating, healing wonder of His holiness subdues and sanctifies you, and the foes of that holiness are banished from your heart.

If I have given to the exegesis of the controlling clause what members of the United States Congress are wont to call an "extension of remarks", it is because the position which Peter takes with respect to the essential *harmlessness* of suffering in the life of the Christian seems to me to require a deeper understanding of Christ's lordship in the Christian's experience. To fumble here is to forfeit a point that is packed with meaning. The behaviour of the Christian who is living "by halves" in respect of Christ's control is not likely to be the same in the

---

[1] A fifth-century monk, Pelagius, denying "original sin", exaggerated and distorted the factor of man's response to God so as to make it appear that by human striving we could make ourselves acceptable to Him.

fierceness of trouble as the behaviour of one who is in fact, for weal or woe, committed to Christ's sovereign reign over his life.

The acknowledgment of this holy sovereignty, says Peter, draws four things in its train:

(a) There is *the immunity it confers*: "WHO IS THERE TO HARM YOU IF YOU ARE ZEALOUS FOR WHAT IS RIGHT? BUT EVEN IF YOU DO SUFFER FOR RIGHTEOUSNESS' SAKE, YOU WILL BE BLESSED" (vv. 13, 14). The exemption, let us observe, is not from *difficulty*, but from *damage*.

The man without faith sees the "harm" in the trouble itself —unpopularity, slander, misrepresentation, ill health, bereavement—whereas the Christian sees nothing as "harm" unless it harms his spirit, his character, his devotion to his Lord.

As long as trouble throws us back on Christ, calls out a stronger trust in Him, challenges to a firmer courage for Him, its threat of harm is averted. More than that, it is *converted*— into assets of beauty and grace.

You have sung H. G. Spafford's hymn "It is Well". But have you sung it knowing its birthplace in a heart of anguish? Spafford was a Christian lawyer in Chicago, whose wife and four young children were at sea in the ill-fated *Ville du Havre*. Colliding with another ship, the *Ville du Havre* went down in twenty minutes. All the children were lost. Mrs. Spafford was picked up from the bone-chilling sea and for two weeks could send no message to her husband. When at last the rescue ship reached the coast of Ireland, she cabled: "Saved alone." In the depths of his bereavement—and at the height of his unshatterable faith—he wrote:

> "*When peace, like a river, attendeth my way,*
> *When sorrows, like sea-billows, roll;*
> *Whatever my lot, Thou hast taught me to say,*
> *It is well, it is well with my soul!*"

Suffering? Yes. Damage? No. "It is *well* with my soul!"

(b) There is *the serenity that it creates*: "HAVE NO FEAR OF
THEM, NOR BE TROUBLED" (v. 14). "You need neither fear
their threats nor worry about them," is the Phillips way of
putting it. Dr. F. B. Meyer, expounding this very passage,
draws three flashing jewels of evidence out of the casket of the
Church's troubled yesterdays. Said one martyr, when sentenced
to die, "I was glad when they said unto me, Let us go into the
house of the Lord." Dear old imperturbable Bunyan, locked
up in Bedford Gaol, set his witness down in verse:

> "*This prison very sweet to me*
> *Hath been since I came here;*
> *And so would also hanging be,*
> *If Thou didst then appear.*"

And for the acme of triumphant composure in distress there
is the instance of the martyr who said, as the faggots were
lighted about him, "Methinks they strew roses at my
feet!"

(c) There is *the testimony it inspires*: "ALWAYS BE PREPARED
TO MAKE A DEFENCE TO ANYONE WHO CALLS YOU TO ACCOUNT
FOR THE HOPE THAT IS IN YOU, YET DO IT WITH GENTLENESS
AND REVERENCE" (v. 15). Greek scholars who are able to deal
with the finer points of vocabulary and style point out a mixing
of suggestions in this sentence. On the one hand, the two words
that are translated "defence" suggest something formal, what
we might call a rational account or explanation. On the other
hand, the verb that is translated "calls" ("asketh" in AV)
"suggests ordinary conversation rather than an official en-
quiry". On the whole it seems best to take this as a piece of
counsel for ordinary members of the Christian community,
most of whom would not be capable of setting forth a theologian's treatise or a logician's argument.

If the "hope that is in you" be taken to include not only the
expectation of future glory, but, as Beare puts it, "The whole
content of the Christian profession" seen as "hope", then we

may think of every true believer filling the role of a witness concerning the Saviour whom he trusts. *This* Christ means to me. *This* I have found since I received Him as my Saviour. *This* I have proved in my own experience.

"That miracle at Cana," said a cynic to a man whom Christ had redeemed from a drunkard's life; "you don't believe that Jesus could turn water into wine, do you?" "I do, sir," said the man. "He surely could do it, for at my house he has been turning whisky into new furniture and new clothes."

A defence to anyone who calls you to account for the hope that is in you! And a good one—given with gentle humour and becoming reverence!

And now it must be seen that a whole-hearted commitment to the Sovereignty of Christ includes one more thing.

(*d*) There is *the sensitivity it produces*: "AND KEEP YOUR CONSCIENCE CLEAR, SO THAT, WHEN YOU ARE ABUSED, THOSE WHO REVILE YOUR GOOD BEHAVIOUR IN CHRIST MAY BE PUT TO SHAME. FOR IT IS BETTER TO SUFFER FOR DOING RIGHT, IF THAT SHOULD BE GOD'S WILL, THAN FOR DOING WRONG" (vv. 16, 17).

In chapter 2, verse 12, Peter has given the directive, "Maintain good conduct." Now we have the same form of address, this time with regard to something that lies behind conduct: "Maintain good conscience." It is the *maintenance* of it that is stressed. For "good" Vincent suggests "unimpaired". It is a useful suggestion, since it is curiously easy to let insensitiveness form like a callus over our conscience, and then to justify this or that kind of behaviour on the false premise that "my conscience is clear".

One commentator, in a burst of eloquence, says, "*Here is the 'charm' for Christians to wear—'a good conscience'. Then to all wrongful treatment of maligning men you can say, 'Strike! you cannot harm. Strike! you may embarrass my circumstances, undermine my health, maim my limbs, rob me of reputation, take away my life; but strike! you cannot harm me.' Such a man*

> '*Can the darkening universe defy*
> *To quench his immortality,*
> *Or shake his faith in God.*' "[1]

Thus far we have examined Peter's appeals to Christians in circumstances of difficulty under two headings: the appeal for behaviour that is consistent with the Christian's integrity and the appeal for behaviour that is committed to Christ's sovereignty. We now come to a third consideration. It must be, says our apostle:

3. *Behaviour that is connected with Calvary's victory.* Spinoza may insist that we must view life *sub specie aeternitatis*, "under the aspect of eternity" (which in itself is a good thing), but Peter keeps hammering it home that Christians must view all of life *sub specie crucis*, "under the aspect of the Cross".

Hence, he says, "FOR CHRIST ALSO DIED FOR SINS ONCE FOR ALL, THE RIGHTEOUS FOR THE UNRIGHTEOUS, THAT HE MIGHT BRING US TO GOD, BEING PUT TO DEATH IN THE FLESH BUT MADE ALIVE IN THE SPIRIT" (v. 18).

Because the three verses that follow—dealing with what the Creed calls Christ's Descent into Hell and with baptism as being somehow linked with Noah's flood—are actually a kind of parenthesis in the flow of Peter's discussion, I want for the moment to separate them out, reserving them for later comment. What is of first importance is to get clearly fixed in our minds the central point that Peter is making. He is addressing himself to the problem of *undeserved suffering*—the righteous suffering at the hands of the unrighteous. This leads him to say, in effect, My brothers, consider our Lord! This was exactly the case with Him. Was He not righteous? Yet look at the pains He bore. Moreover, He suffered to the limit—even unto death.

But death was not the end. He conquered death, rose from

[1] U. R. Thomas, in *The Pulpit Commentary*, vol. on "Peter, John, Jude" (Funk and Wagnalls, New York), p. 160.

the dead, and (now moving to verse 22) "HAS GONE INTO HEAVEN AND IS AT THE RIGHT HAND OF GOD, WITH ANGELS, AUTHORITIES, AND POWERS SUBJECT TO HIM".

I am not suggesting that the intervening verses are without value. They must have their point and purpose, else Peter would not have offered the observations they contain, full of perplexity though they are. What I am suggesting is that endless arguments and a million words about the meaning of "the spirits in prison" and "baptism doth also now save us" must not be permitted to lure us from the main road of Peter's presentation. The chief thought here is the link between unmerited suffering in the life of the Church (or of the individual believer) and the Calvary passion of our Lord. If we fail to see this, we lose our scent and miss our quarry.

With this point fastened down, as I trust it is in all our minds, we turn, because honour-bound to do so, to the in-between verses, where the minds of the fanciful have conjured up some astonishing pictures and the minds of the most restrainedly serious have done an enormous amount of wrestling with difficulties. If one has an ounce of modesty in him, he will concede at the outset the impossibility of offering an exposition that satisfies everyone.

First of all, what does Peter *say* in these verses (19–21)?

He says that Jesus, being "put to death in the flesh but made alive in the spirit", "went and preached to the spirits in prison".

He says of these "spirits in prison" that they "formerly did not obey when God's patience waited in the days of Noah, during the building of the ark".

He says that in the ark "eight persons were saved through water".

He says that "baptism", which corresponds to this, "now saves you . . . through the resurrection of Jesus Christ".

This, so far at least as it can be conveyed in the English language of the *Revised Standard Version*, is what Peter *says*.

The obvious question follows: what does Peter *mean*?

The division of interpretation on the "spirits in prison" passage is at least fourfold, whereas the division of opinion concerning the "baptism" passage is really only twofold.

Regarding the former there are the following positions that have been taken:

1. The preaching to which Peter refers was done by Christ through the Holy Spirit in the ministry of Noah and others prior to the Flood. Those who are now "spirits in prison" *then* had their chance to repent and refused to do so. Some illustrious names are associated with this interpretation, such as Thomas Aquinas, Archbishop Leighton, John Lightfoot, and Professor Salmond.

2. The preaching was by Christ to the dead, was done between His death and His resurrection, and it included not only the generation who came to their end in Noah's flood but the dead generally, the wider inclusion being based on I Peter 4: 6, where it is said that "the gospel was preached even to the dead". Owing to the fact that the word for "preach" in 3: 19 means *heralding* or *proclaiming* (and is only used sometimes for preaching the Gospel) and the word so translated in 4: 6 is consistently employed for the announcement of the good news of salvation, holders of this view are themselves divided. Some, who feel that one verse throws light upon the other, make this the basis for what has come to be called the Larger Hope, or what others call (not accurately perhaps) a Second Chance.

Some, on the other hand, who give to 4: 6 a meaning of its own, regard the announcement by the crucified Jesus as an occasion of release and assurance for the righteous dead of the Old Testament times, the reference to the disobedience of Noah's day serving only to heighten the fact that the number of the obedient, namely eight, was extremely small. This is in substance John Calvin's view. (It may be noted that others go further with this idea of good news for the righteous dead of olden times, linking it with St. Paul's word in Ephesians 4: 8 and with the notion that the abode of the dead was now to be altered, the holy dead of the past to be released from Sheol

into the heights of God's presence and the righteous dead there-
after to join them, immediately on decease, and to be, as St.
Paul would put it, "present with the Lord".)

3. That the preaching was indeed the proclaiming of the
Gospel, and that it was the preaching of Christ by the Holy
Spirit through the apostles (notably Peter), and that the
"spirits in prison" were living men held fast in the bondage of
their sins, the reference to Noah having the effect of showing the
contrast between the small results of his preaching and the
tremendous effects of the apostolic preaching, as for example
on the Day of Pentecost. This seems to have been the view
of the beloved evangelical teacher and expositor, Dr. Griffith
Thomas.

4. The fourth view, as now given, is the one with which I
would associate myself: (1) The preaching was a proclamation
of victory; (2) was made by our Lord Himself in the non-
corporeal mode of His existence on which He entered immediately at death (when indeed His "spirit" was "quickened",
released, triumphant, and He was not "straitened" as He said
He was in approaching His Cross); (3) the "spirits in prison"
were the fallen angels alluded to in Genesis 6: 1–8, whose
seductive powers over earthly women are connected with the
ghastly wickedness of antediluvian society, these apostate
angelic beings having the same identity as those referred to in
II Peter 2: 4, who have been "delivered into chains of darkness";
(4) that this announcement of victory to these particularly
defiant and destructive angels fits in with Peter's thought that
the crucified and risen Lord is in fact the Lord of all, "with
angels, authorities, and powers subject to him" (3: 19).

The discussion of this strange and perplexing passage could
be extended at great length. The available literature on it is
voluminous. One must say, regretfully, that no consensus
as to its interpretation appears anywhere on the horizon.[1]

[1] For an extraordinarily thorough and illuminating discussion of the whole
problem the reader is referred both to the exegetical notes and Essay I in the
appendix of Selwyn's *The First Epistle of Peter* (Macmillan and Co., New York:
1961), pp. 195–203, 313–62.

Let us pass on to the "baptism" section of the parenthetical verses we have under review.

The reference to Noah's generation suggests to Peter the story of the ark and the safety with which Noah and his family were brought through the judgment of the Flood. In that ark, he tells us, were eight persons who were "saved through water" (v. 20). That is, they "were brought in safety through the water", as a number of translators have it. Our apostle then proceeds to say, "BAPTISM, WHICH CORRESPONDS TO THIS, NOW SAVES YOU, NOT AS REMOVAL OF DIRT FROM THE BODY BUT AS AN APPEAL TO GOD FOR A CLEAR CONSCIENCE THROUGH THE RESUR-RECTION OF JESUS CHRIST" (v. 21).

Several points emerge at once: (1) the waters of the Flood are somehow a type, a prefiguring, an illustration, of Christian baptism; (2) the baptism is somehow a counterpart, an "anti-type" (which is a literal rendering of the Greek word) of the waters that bore up the ark; (3) the water of Christian baptism, however, does not of itself cleanse anything, its significance being spiritual; (4) that to which it testifies in the form of a pledge to God is a good conscience; (5) this meaning of baptism as a witness to our salvation has validity only as it is related to the risen Christ and to the new life which He by the Holy Spirit imparts on the ground of His atoning death for us.

Roman Catholic teaching uniformly looks to this passage as one of its "proof texts" in support of "baptismal regenera-tion". The same cannot be said for the Anglican community (which of course includes our American Episcopalians), some within it holding strongly to the words of the Baptismal Service, "Seeing now that this child is regenerate", while others, such as Bishop J. C. Ryle, apply what he calls the principle of "charitable supposition" to this and other parts of the Prayer Book, refusing to affirm that any outward rite of the Church can of itself guarantee the operation of the grace of God.

Perhaps it should be added that in the United States some groups, which recognize the validity of none but *believer's baptism*, teach nevertheless that in the submission to this ordinance the candidate is in fact regenerated. This is mentioned because the view taken by the Disciples of Christ Church, for example, differs from the familiar one maintained by the Baptist bodies, where the ordinance *follows*, and is a witness to, the new life received through faith in Jesus Christ.

In taking leave of this controversial portion of Peter's epistle let me quote, with approval and appreciation, a sentence from Professor Alan Stibbs of Oak Hill College, London. In his commentary on these verses, which, I must say, is excellent throughout, he says of Peter's reference to baptism: "The hope of the benefit thus figuratively pledged being vitally realized in the sinner's experience is not to be found in any power in the baptism ceremony, or in the baptismal water, to wash away the filth of the flesh; but in a sincere response of heart to God, and particularly in one's personal confession of faith in Christ crucified and risen."[1]

Our remarks have been long enough to require now a moment of review and orientation as we get back to the main current of the apostle's thought. The subject under discussion is the conduct of Christians in circumstances of difficulty, especially of opposition and persecution. In such circumstances their deportment, as we have seen, must be consistent with that integrity of character which marks the Christian and it must be committed always to the sovereignty of Christ reigning within the heart.

The third requirement in such deportment, introduced at verse 18, is that it must be *connected in some vital way with Christ's triumph in His death and resurrection*. The transitional key is in the words, "CHRIST ALSO DIED . . . THE RIGHTEOUS FOR THE UNRIGHTEOUS" (v. 18).

Note the force of "also". You are suffering unjustly; so did He. You for a righteous cause are being assailed by unrighteous men; so was He.

---

[1] Alan M. Stibbs, *The First Epistle General of Peter* (Wm. B. Eerdmans, Grand Rapids; Tyndale Press, London).

Behold, cries Peter, the connection between your situation and His!

Now what exactly is the connection?

We must see it, I think, as twofold:

(a) Our sufferings are connected with Calvary's victorious suffering *as a lesson is connected with those who learn it.* Note verse 1 of chapter 4, which is well drawn out in the NEB: "REMEMBERING THAT CHRIST ENDURED BODILY SUFFERING, YOU MUST ARM YOURSELVES WITH A TEMPER OF MIND LIKE HIS." At this level of meaning the verse signifies the same thought that Peter has already expressed in 2 : 21 : "CHRIST ALSO SUFFERED FOR YOU, LEAVING YOU AN EXAMPLE, THAT YOU SHOULD FOLLOW IN HIS STEPS." The helmet and shield of the Christian is a frame of mind in which trouble, in some degree or another, is taken for granted. Trouble is something to be meekly and uncomplainingly borne, creatively and victoriously used, and, throughout, is to occasion a courageous following in the steps of that Prince of Pain, Jesus Christ the Lord.

Peter and Charles Wesley would clasp hands over this:

> "*Soldiers of Christ, arise,*
> *And put your armour on,*
> *Strong in the strength which God supplies*
> *Through His eternal Son;*
> *Strong in the Lord of Hosts,*
> *And in His mighty power,*
> *Who in the strength of Jesus trusts*
> *Is more than conqueror.*"[1]

But Peter would take us deeper as he forges the link between our pains and the triumphant pains of the crucified Lord.

(b) Our sufferings are connected with His, not only as a lesson is connected with those who learn it, *but as a life is connected with those who share it*: "SINCE THEREFORE CHRIST

---

[1] Charles Wesley, "Soldiers of Christ, Arise", printed in the *Keswick Hymn-Book* (Marshall, Morgan and Scott, London), No. 246.

SUFFERED IN THE FLESH, ARM YOURSELVES WITH THE SAME
THOUGHT, FOR WHOEVER HAS SUFFERED IN THE FLESH HAS
CEASED FROM SIN, SO AS TO LIVE FOR THE REST OF THE TIME IN
THE FLESH NO LONGER BY HUMAN PASSIONS BUT BY THE WILL OF
GOD" (4: 1, 2).

In his outline notes on *I Peter*, Dr. Griffith Thomas remarks on
this passage, "It is Peter's equivalent of Paul's teaching in
Romans 6." This I believe to be the clue to the deep and
important truth here set forth.

(1) We therefore have, first of all, the *complete identification*.
To see a *similarity* between the Suffering Saviour and ourselves
has its value of encouragement. Far more important, however,
is the discovery of the *peculiarity* in the relationship between
the crucified Lord and ourselves. That peculiarity, according
to Paul and Peter, becomes by faith an identity: He dying for
us and we dying with Him, He rising again for us and we rising
with Him, He ascending and reigning for us and we ascending
and reigning with Him.

What appears to give special relevance to St. Paul's treatment
of this theme in Romans 6 is the fact that Christian baptism
is in the back of Paul's mind even as it is here in the case of
Peter. "Do you not know," he asks, "that all of us who have
been baptized into Christ Jesus were baptized into his death?
We were buried therefore with him by baptism into death, so
that as Christ was raised from the dead by the glory of the
Father, we too might walk in newness of life" (vv. 3, 4).

Here, clearly, the principle of the believer's identification
with Christ is laid down.

Now let us go on with St. Paul, using the translation of the
NEB, which here on the whole I very much like: "*For if we
have become incorporate with him in a death like his we shall also
be one with him in a resurrection like his. We know that the man
we once were has been crucified with Christ, for the destruction of
the sinful self, so that we may no longer be the slaves of sin, since
a dead man is no longer answerable for his sin.*" (*The RSV reads:
"For he who has died is freed from sin.*") "*But if we thus died*

with Christ we believe that we shall also come to life with him. We know that Christ, once raised from the dead, is never to die again: he is no longer under the dominion of death. For in dying as he died, he died to sin once for all, and in living as he lives, he lives to God. In the same way, you must regard yourselves as dead to sin and alive to God, in union with Christ Jesus" (vv. 5–11).

Three leading ideas are joined in this remarkable passage: finality, identity, and liberty. There was *finality* about that death which Christ died, in order, as Peter would say, to "bring us to God" (3 : 18). He doesn't go on dying forever. "He has appeared once for all at the end of the age to put away sin by the sacrifice of himself" (Hebrews 9: 26). It is a strong New Testament emphasis.

Blended with this thought of finality is the idea of *identity*. St. Paul declares that God's intention in Christ for His people is a faith-union (*spiritual* rather than *metaphysical*) between them and Him in which their whole identity as alien, guilty, self-willed members of the lost human community is given up, renounced, abandoned, and a new identity in the new community of the redeemed is given to them. This new identity is such that, as God sees them, and as they see themselves, they are *in Christ*. They are *in Christ* for everything: not just as an escape from hell, but as their righteousness, their holiness, their peace, their power, their hope, their victory.

Joined with the thought of finality and identity is the attractive truth of *liberty*. This identification with the crucified and risen Lord means that the redeemed are "freed from sin". They are rendered capable, through the Christ with whom this identification of faith has been established, of responding to the uncompromising directive, "Let not sin *therefore* reign in your mortal bodies" (Romans 6: 12).

Now it is my conviction that when we have grasped this truth, when our insight into the apostolic teaching of the believer's identification with Christ, has probed deep enough to reach the nerve of the truth, we are prepared to understand Peter's strong word: "*Since therefore Christ suffered in the flesh, arm yourselves with the same thought, for whoever has suffered in the flesh has ceased from sin.*" With Peter, "suffered" is the equivalent of "death". That is to say, whoever in this mortal life has accepted his place of death with Christ, with knowledge of its implications and privileges, has thereby accepted the principle that sin and sinning are not for him.

Sin in will, sin in habit, sin in disposition—the whole business is to be jettisoned. In union with Christ the soul is engaged in the higher business of righteousness.

To be sure, this strong putting of the matter leaves some phases of the redeemed life undiscussed—the place and treatment of specific sins into which Christians, normally victorious, may fall, the mysterious depths of human nature which psychiatry has unquestionably opened up to us, the hinterland of the "unconscious" where instinctual and emotional factors operate *sub rosa* to sway our thoughts and actions, the whole range of omissions in the "never, never land" of what we might have done—these remain to humble us and to set the pattern of progressive sanctification long after the occurrence of whatever crisis God has put us through to show us the "way of holiness" in union with His Holy Son.

The truth here is paradox indeed. Apart from Him, wretched; in Him, blessed! Apart from Him, unholy; in Him, clean! Apart from Him, frazzled and frustrated; in Him, competent and steadfast! Apart from Him, vanquished; in Him, victorious! Apart from Him, terrified; in Him, dauntless!

Christopher Wordsworth saw this, felt it, believed it, sang it:

> "*He has raised our human nature*
> *In the clouds to God's right hand;*
> *There we sit in heavenly places,*
> *There with Him in glory stand:*
> *Jesus reigns, adored by angels;*
> *Man with God is on the throne;*
> *Mighty Lord, in Thine ascension*
> *We by faith behold our own.*

Glory be to God the Father,
  Glory be to God the Son,
Dying, risen, ascending for us,
  Who the heavenly realm has won;
Glory to the Holy Spirit
  To One God in Persons Three,
Glory both in earth and heaven
  Glory, endless glory be!"

'Will you remember this?' says Peter, to his troubled brethren. Will you see this connection between your difficulties and what your Lord has made possible for you in dying and rising? Will you conduct yourselves as those who accept, in fact and experience, their place of identification with the holy, conquering Redeemer?

If you will, then something inevitably follows. You have already begun to discover it.

(2) The complete identification always creates the *clear demarcation* : "LET THE TIME THAT IS PAST SUFFICE FOR DOING THAT WHICH THE GENTILES LIKE TO DO, LIVING IN LICENTIOUS-NESS, PASSIONS, DRUNKENNESS, REVELS, CAROUSING, AND LAW-LESS IDOLATRY" (v. 3).

There is in fact a double contrast or difference here. To get the first part of it you need only this third verse. "Let the time that is past suffice", or, better still in Moffatt, "you have given time enough in the past", for "doing what the Gentiles like to do". Here is the contrast between the Church and society, between the believer and the world.

The Greek word for "Gentiles" is not a proper name, at all. It is a term that may be translated "nations", or, even more literally, *ethnic groups*. The word "ethnic" is derived from it. We are not off target if we ask ourselves as Christians: Do our nation, our national culture, our contemporary mores and customs, determine our conduct in decisive ways? Or is our behaviour governed by the mind of Jesus Christ, let society say what it will?

One night I sat with a family of friends in London as a special "newscast" was being done on television. Thousands of young people had been having a sort of jamboree somewhere in the Midlands. It was a jazz festival. A roving reporter had gone with his "mike" to ask questions of first one and then another of these young folks. Such merry-making as was shown on the television screen was silly enough, but it was not what Peter calls "licentious", the Greek word being in plural form and meaning "open outrages against decency" (the BBC's own sense of decency would see to that!). But then came the answers these "teens" and "twenties" gave to the questions that were put to them. "Statistics show," said the reporter, "that at the time of their marriage one out of five young women in England is already pregnant. Do you see anything wrong in this?" One after another the answers came, from both sexes, "No, I see nothing wrong with this."

More and more, the name, "Christian" is being outmoded in the culture of the nations of the West. More and more, therefore, the Church needs to take seriously the New Testament message on the line of demarcation that passes between the community of the redeemed and the society of the nation.

One word of warning: God forgive us if we who say we are among the redeemed are merely smug about it. What we need is not less contact with society's pagans and wastrels, but more! No compromise, but huge quantities of contacts! Less blowing off of the steam of our indignation against them and more harnessing of our energies for bold, patient, imaginative Christian witness to these youngsters whom Christ would save and then command in a life of thrilling adventure!

To get the second form of the contrast we need the next verse: "THEY ARE SURPRISED THAT YOU DO NOT NOW JOIN THEM IN THE SAME WILD PROFLIGACY" (v. 4). Take four words out of verse 3, "time that is past", and two words out of verse 4, "not now".

"Time that is past!"

"Not now!"

And how describe the difference?

"Past": "doing what the Gentiles like to do!" (v. 3).

"Now": doing "the will of God" (v. 2). "FOR THIS IS WHY THE GOSPEL WAS PREACHED" (Greek—"the Good News was proclaimed"), EVEN TO THE DEAD, THAT THOUGH JUDGED IN THE FLESH LIKE MEN (as mortals subject to death), THEY MIGHT LIVE IN THE SPIRIT LIKE GOD" (v. 6).

Her name—Elizabeth Burns—can be freely used, for she has committed it to the public in a book that has had a wide circulation in the United States. Breezily entitled *The Late Liz*, it is the unusual testimony of a modern pagan who underwent a tremendous Christian conversion. With three shattered marriages behind her, with a spirit that was ulcerous with bitterness and a mind that was numb from bruising, she one night downed thirteen high-potency sleeping tablets. The attempt at suicide came within a hair of succeeding. Christ found her in a hospital, where she was recovering. What happened is best told in her own words:

"The world in which I lay was a very private world, and I was quite alone. And then, all at once, I was not alone. There was no increase in light, no sound, no motion, no scent. Lying utterly still I waited. Unable to accept it, I was now accepting, letting myself be claimed, letting this something mount and permeate and cover the self I'd been, as the tide rises to cover what was formerly dry and bare. And now I knew what this was, this was the Father, here was the Glory of the patient Presence. Wonder came, and with the wonder, peace—not the peace the world knows but an in-going, at-one-ness; and I understood, I understood that I had been forgiven."[1]

The fact that she moved in the "high" circles of America's moneyed class had not kept her from the agonies of alcoholism.

---

[1] Elizabeth Burns, *The Late Liz* (Appleton-Century-Crofts, New York: 1957), p. 172.

But now Christ had replaced the old torment with His own tranquillity. Since then she has gone on from strength to strength.

Peter would understand. So would many of these converted pagans who would read his letter.

"Time that is past": "doing what the Gentiles like to do!"

"Now": "doing the will of God!"

"But what if the old life never was like that?" you ask. Obviously the transformation will have no such outward or dramatic character as this one. Still and all, the comment of Professor Stibbs is valid in its own way: "Earthly life becomes divided for the Christian into *the time past*, before his conversion, and *the rest of his time in the flesh* (v. 2), after his conversion."[1]

(3) Finally, besides the complete identification and the characteristic demarcation, there is the *consequent opposition* that is often associated with that life which is lived in union with His life. "AND THEY ABUSE YOU" (v. 4) is the brief, blunt clause that Peter frames to tell it. When Phillips translates the Greek here as "they say all sorts of unpleasant things about you", he is putting forward the kind of understatement for which the English are said to be famous. Actually, says Peter, they *blaspheme* your name; they revile and defame you.

Julius was an old soldier of Rome who had become a Christian. Hailed before Maximus the judge, he was charged with the capital offence of refusing longer to worship Caesar. "What a fool you are," said Maximus scornfully, "to make more of a crucified man than of a living emperor!" But "He died for our sins that He might give us eternal life," replied Julius. "Sacrifice and then live!" said the contemptuous Maximus. "If I choose life," answered the old veteran, "I choose death; if I die, I live for ever." At that, the judge lost his temper, and sentenced him to death.[2]

As for a man like Maximus, and for those of his ilk, Peter would say, "THEY WILL GIVE ACCOUNT TO HIM WHO IS READY TO JUDGE THE LIVING AND THE DEAD" (v. 5).

---

[1] Stibbs, *Ibid.*, p. 149.
[2] Workman, *Ibid.*, p. 40.

As for you Christians, he would say, Continue to deport yourselves as men of courage, without bitterness or revenge. You may not experience death at all—will not in fact if Christ comes again soon enough. But many Christians have died and, dying, they have gone through that (for them) last manifestation of God's judgment on the sin of mankind, since, as St. Paul has it, "death came by sin, and so death passed upon all men" (Romans 5: 12). "FOR THIS IS WHY THE GOSPEL WAS PREACHED EVEN TO THE DEAD, THAT THOUGH JUDGED IN THE FLESH LIKE MEN (AS MORTALS SUBJECT TO DEATH) THEY MIGHT LIVE IN THE SPIRIT LIKE GOD" (v. 6).

It must in fairness be said that there are one or two alternatives of construction here. Such is the arrangement of the words in the Greek text that some scholars read "that they might be judged by men with respect to their physical existence". In this case the reference is to Christian martyrs and others who have been judged, condemned, and sentenced, by hostile men. Though men killed them, the true life that was in them through the gospel was God's life—eternal.

The word for "life" here is not the same as that which Peter has used in verse 2. There it is the life of the Christian, to be sure, but it is his life as *related to the body*, therefore mortal, transitory, perishable. Here it is life as *related to God* through the Holy Spirit—everlasting, indestructible.

Let us cast our eye backward over what we have been saying. How the Christian is to behave in the presence of trouble, how he is to conduct himself in relation to those who oppose him—this has been Peter's topic in the section of the letter we have had under inspection.

This behaviour asks for three things: that it be steadily consistent with the Christian's integrity, that it be single-mindedly committed to Christ's sovereignty over life, and that it be significantly connected with the victory Christ has won for us at Calvary.

The section ends, as we have just seen, on the high note of the life eternal, a possession from Christ so surely held and so highly prized that it turns trouble into triumph and night into day.

> *"And when the strife is fierce, the warfare long,*
> *Steals on the ear the distant triumph-song*
> *And hearts are brave again, and arms are strong.*
> *Alleluia!"*

V

ALERTED AGAINST DANGER

V

ALERTED AGAINST DANGER

"*The life of the individual Christian*," says Bishop Stephen Neil, "*will always be marked by conflict and temptation. Each age, each stage of life, has its own problems, its own pitfalls, its own subtle occasions of failure. It is usually supposed that youth is the period of most dangerous temptations. I would rather say it is the time of the most obvious temptation. The besetting weakness of middle age is self-complacency and unadventurous acceptance of things as they are. The besetting weakness of old age is an unwillingness to accept the fact of being old . . . an inner querulousness about life as God has made it, self-pity, a kind of resentment against the young . . . and a consequent refusal to see any good in anything that is new.*"

He then goes on to remark that "the existence of all these possibilities of failure is a reminder, if any reminder is still needed, that Christian holiness involves an ever-repeated self-commitment to the exacting demands of the holiness of God in ever-changing situations".[1]

The mood in which the bishop writes is precisely the mood of the Apostle Peter in the concluding section of his letter, to which we now turn.

As all the way along, he is still exhorting, still pleading, still counselling. It might be added that there is some repetition of things already mentioned. Having followed him through those appeals that are linked pre-eminently with the *privileges* of the people of God and those that are linked with the *practices* of the people of God, we are ready for the final cycle of entreaties.

[1] Stephen Neil, *Christian Holiness* (Lutterworth Press, London: 1960), pp. 104, 105.

III. APPEALS THAT ARE LINKED WITH THE PERILS OF THE PEOPLE OF GOD: 4:7—5:11

For Christians who are beset and beleaguered there are hazards. There are, to use the bishop's word, "pitfalls". In bitter experience Peter had found this for himself. He would therefore sound an alert.

Remember this, he writes, "THE END OF ALL THINGS IS AT HAND" (v. 7). Theologians use the word "eschatology" when they wish to speak of things future and final: death, the Lord's return, judgment, heaven and hell. The eschatology of the New Testament is a fascinating thing to study, holding far more wonders than most Christians realize who read only the books on prophecy of one school of thought. As with matters of election or sanctification, Holy Scripture is written with an enormously fertile freedom, untrammelled by the often denuding exactitudes of theories and schemes that men *will* impose on what is revealed.

One thing on which the New Testament insists is that the "end" in God's purposes is both a *termination* and a *consummation*. Nor does it occur in what we call a "day"—a 24-hour span. It occurs in one of God's "times", answering the Greek word *chairos*, which means a time of importance, of crucial significance. Within it, to be sure, may be particular moments of events and occurrence, as when "suddenly" the heavenly chorus was heard by the shepherds at Bethlehem or when "suddenly" the Holy Spirit descended at Pentecost. Acknowledging such a circumstance, however, does not alter the point that God's endings and beginnings are of the nature of crucial processes, not simply momentary flashes.

Thus, for example, from one point of view the "end" of the dispensation that we know as the Old Testament, or Old Covenant, began when Jesus, the Messiah and Saviour, in the fullness of time, came to our world. From another point of view it came to an end when he died upon the Cross, with the words "It is finished" upon his lips, and the veil of the temple was

torn from the top to the bottom. From still another point of
view it came to an end when, a whole generation later, the
Temple was destroyed and the Holy City laid in ruins. Jesus
had said, "Truly I say to you, there will not be left here one
stone upon another, that will not be beaten down" (Matthew
24: 2).

Now from *this* point of view the old order, though doomed,
did not in fact end until A.D. 70 in the destruction of Jerusalem.
From this point of view that for which the Temple stood, the
Old Covenant of works and sacrifice, did not finally pass away
until then. It was therefore still future, though extremely
near—perhaps half a dozen years away—at the time of Peter's
writing.

While I have no right to claim his support for this view of
Peter's reference to "the end", let me nevertheless, in confirmation of the larger thought which I have brought forward,
quote from Bishop Marcus Loane in his exposition of Hebrews
9: 26:

"'*But now once in the end of the world hath he appeared to
put away sin by the sacrifice of himself.' Thus,*" says Loane,
"*His self-offering is looked upon as a terminal point in the long
succession of the ages; it marks the close of 'a long and com-
plex course of finite development!' . . . (quoted from Westcott)
and it refers to the end as something other than just a fact. It is
meant to convey the idea of consummation, an end that brings
many parts to ultimate fruition. The death of Christ with His
exaltation to God's right hand represents a new departure to
the course of history, and it took place once for all at the close of
the ages to mark the dawn of a new day.*"[1]

Termination? Yes. But more, consummation—a fulfilment
that leads on to a larger unfolding!

If this principle of New Testament eschatology is recognized,

[1] Marcus L. Loane, *Key Texts in the Epistle to the Hebrews* (Marshall, Morgan,
& Scott, London: 1961), p. 87.

then we are prepared to see that the first advent of our Lord brought an old order to an end by consummating the purposes of God in and for that order, and thus introducing a new order, the order of "the Kingdom of his beloved Son, in whom we have redemption, the forgiveness of sins" (Colossians 1 : 13, 14).

In this order, which has a certain finality about it, the victory of Christ over sin and death and Satan is not something to which we look *forward*. The victory has already been won— at the Cross and in the Resurrection. Sin *was* "put away". Satan *was* judged. Death *was* overcome.

What then remains? What is yet ahead? Much indeed. But it will not be the *winning* of the victory of Christ; it will be the *exhibiting* of that victory. It will not be the introduction of His reign over "Angels, authorities, and powers"; it will be the finalizing of it.

And that "end", still to be fulfilled, will usher in still larger unfoldings of God's purposes for His Church and for His world. That end, moreover, is repeatedly set before the Church by New Testament writers as something imminent, an event at hand, a coming of the Lord for which His people are to be ever watching. As the saintly Lancelot Andrews has it, in a para-phrase of the Lord's Prayer, "Let Thy kingdom come to me here in the state of grace, that I may come in to it in the state of glory."[1] We are to abide in the one; we are watchfully to anticipate the other.

Wise and experienced Peter, however, knows full well how easy it is for Christians to lose their vigilance and zest. He therefore points out:

A. The peril of *complacency*: since "THE END OF ALL THINGS IS AT HAND", you must "KEEP SANE AND SOBER" (v. 7). "Culti-vate sobriety and alertness of spirit," is Beare's excellent rendering of it. Helpful too is the translation of the *Amplified New Testament*: "Keep sound-minded and self-restrained and alert." There are specific danger-zones, Peter suggests, over which complacency can steal like some contagious stupor:

[1] Quoted by Selwyn, *Ibid.*, p. 113.

1. The Christian is in peril if *prayer is perfunctory*: "KEEP SANE AND SOBER FOR YOUR PRAYERS" (v. 7). "What is wrong with us," cries A. J. Gossip, with that impassioned eloquence which was so natural with him, "what is wrong with us that in the average life the flame of worship has sunk so low, and burns so dimly; that whereas Jesus Christ was constant in communion with His Father; felt the need of it, and exulted in the joy of it; walked with God and talked to God; knew He was never alone because the Father was with Him; and so came through that disappointing life of His in that glory of gallantry and unsullied honour, so many nowadays of those He died to save feel little or no impulse to all that; and neither think of practising it at all, or do so only in a hurried perfunctory fashion."[1]

There it is, fairly trumpeted to our attention—this danger of letting prayer slowly stiffen into a frosty form.

2. The Christian is in peril if *love is lax*: "ABOVE ALL, HOLD UNFAILING YOUR LOVE FOR ONE ANOTHER, SINCE LOVE COVERS A MULTITUDE OF SINS" (v. 8). There is no point in being watchful about the fellowship with God that we find in prayer unless we are, at the same time, vigilant to maintain at full pitch that brotherly love which binds us to others in the body of Christ.

The adjective "unfailing" is well rendered "at full strength" in the *New English Bible*. The Greek word, as Cranfield points out, suggests "the taut muscle of strenuous and sustained effort as of an athlete".[2] Our apostle, having used the word in 1: 22, returns to it here, where it has essentially the same meaning as in St. Paul's plea that the Ephesian believers should be "forbearing" toward one another in love, "eager to maintain the unity of the Spirit in the bond of peace" (4: 2, 3).

In the Evangelical Awakening in the eighteenth century in England John Fletcher and John Berridge were on opposite sides of the controversy over Calvinism and Arminianism. Each one wrote openly against the views maintained by the other.

---

[1] Gossip, *In the Secret Place of the Most High* (Independent Press, Ltd., London: 1946), pp. 13, 14.
[2] Cranfield, *Ibid.*, p. 57.

Berridge, out of his element as a controversialist, gave up the attack. Fletcher, gracious even towards those whom he differed with most sharply, carried on. Yet when the two men met, after not seeing each other for some years, they embraced each other with both arms, as Berridge exclaimed, "My dear brother!"

Says Marcus Loane, in recording the incident, "Never did two spirits of more kindred joy meet with each other, and for two hours they were absorbed in most affectionate conversation. Then they took to their knees, while each joined in prayer of the most warm and tender spirit; it seemed almost as if they could not bear to part."[1]

Peter's spirit would have leaped for joy at a sight so Christian!

Love has a built-in "stretch-out" for meeting circumstances that are awkward and difficult.

As for the proverbial saying that it "covers a multitude of sins", it seems best to understand this in reference to the very point that came out in Peter's exchange with his Master on the day the question was brought up, "How often shall my brother sin against me, and I forgive him?" Peter suggested "seven times" as a generous figure. Jesus multiplied that by seventy, meaning, thereby, that it was to be multiplied indefinitely.

3. The Christian is in peril *if hospitality is without heart*: "PRACTICE HOSPITALITY UNGRUDGINGLY TO ONE ANOTHER" (v. 9). Most exactly the adverb would read "unmurmuringly". It is a tonal word that suggests its own meaning: leave off the *grumbling*.

There were good reasons for the repeated New Testament stress on the grace of hospitality. Hotels were unknown in those days. Inns were few and far between. Christians who travelled wanted—and needed—the fellowship of their Christian brothers and sisters. Not only was hospitality required by private persons but also by the little groups of Christians, who, without church buildings, had to meet in ordinary dwellings.

[1] Marcus L. Loane, *Cambridge and the Evangelical Succession* (Lutterworth Press, London: 1952), p. 99.

The records indicate, thrillingly enough, that hospitality was so generously practised as to pave the way for impostors. It became necessary for travelling members of the Christian community to carry credentials in order that eager and open-hearted hosts might not have criminal advantage taken of them. What an outpouring of the spirit of brotherhood, charity, and good-will!

Yet occasionally, perhaps where unusual demands had been made upon family facilities and comforts, a complaining mood would be generated. Watch against that, says Peter. Suppose it were your Lord Himself that came upon your doorstep!

4. The Christian is in peril *if ministry is meagre*: "AS EACH HAS RECEIVED A GIFT, EMPLOY IT FOR ONE ANOTHER, AS GOOD STEWARDS OF GOD'S VARIED GRACE" (V. 10).

Instead of grumbling there should be graciousness! Don't ever complain over any giving, or giving up, that you do for Christ's sake and the sake of your brethren. Rather, see to it that whatever gift or capability God has entrusted to you is used to the full for the benefit of the whole community of believers.

Each of us *has* had a gift laid in his hands, thanks to the grace of God. Can any of us doubt it who has ever read Romans 12 or I Corinthians 12? Prophesying, teaching, pastoring, exhorting, healing, helping, making offerings, administering—somewhere in this catalogue of *charisms*, this blessed inventory of special capabilities that are the sovereign bestowal of the Holy Spirit, you and I have a share.

Are we taking our trust seriously? Are we dispensing our Master's "goods" with a large-souled faithfulness, such as befits His overflowing heart, or are we indifferent and pre-occupied, rendering, if anything at all, only a pinched and parsimonious service? "The steward," as Selwyn reminds us, "was responsible to the master of the house for distributing to the other members of the household their shares of his stores."[1] The steward owned nothing; he dispensed all.

[1] Selwyn, *Ibid.*, p. 218.

When all members of the Church of our Lord are doing service, each with his special gift, the effect is that of a symphony in which may be heard and felt "the magnificently varied grace of God" (Phillips). The Greek word for "varied", observes Beare, in a choice comment, "suggests both richness and infinite variety, with an undertone of the harmonious beauty which is exhibited in the union of the different gifts".[1]

This ministry, Peter goes on to point out, takes two forms: speech and action. Regarding the first, he says, "WHOEVER SPEAKS," let him do it "AS ONE WHO UTTERS THE ORACLES OF GOD". Regarding action, he lays it down, "WHOEVER RENDERS SERVICE, AS ONE WHO RENDERS IT BY THE STRENGTH WHICH GOD SUPPLIES" (v. 11).

In both cases it is God who really makes authentic and effective what His servant does. The preacher, for example, is not to speak as if he himself were an oracle, overflowing with a kind of garrulous cleverness. He is to preach as a man who knows that God has spoken to him (and to the Church) in Holy Scripture and by the Holy Spirit. It is his responsibility to transmit God's message in reliance upon God's resources. And God's message, whatever may be the variations in our approach to it and our application of it, always has something to say about His Son our Lord who took our sins and bore them in His own body on the Cross. If that is omitted, what is left, be it never so eloquent, is just what Tennyson calls in *In Memoriam* "vacant chaff well-meant for grain".

Keep awake, says Peter. Avoid complacency as you would the plague. If your *prayers are honest, your love intense, your hospitality ungrudging, your ministry (whether words or deeds) generous and faithful*, then God will be "glorified", as He should be "in everything", through Jesus Christ our Lord. "TO HIM BELONG GLORY AND DOMINION FOR EVER AND EVER" (v. 11).

From this appeal for watchfulness in view of the peril of complacency, Peter turns to another danger in the life of God's people.

[1] Beare, *Ibid.*, p. 160.

B. There is the peril of *consternation*.

Using again the tender, solicitous vocative "Beloved", the apostle pleads, admonishingly, "DO NOT BE SURPRISED AT THE FIERY ORDEAL WHICH COMES UPON YOU TO PROVE YOU, AS THOUGH SOMETHING STRANGE WERE HAPPENING TO YOU" (v. 12).

Scholars, to whom we owe much, are nevertheless capable of curious twists and biases. Professor Francis Beare makes much of this expression "the fiery ordeal", which, when linked with Peter's reference to the "name of Christ" in v. 14, he assumes to mean a period when throughout the Roman Empire it was a crime simply to bear the name "Christian". On the ground that the "crime" of being a Christian was not the basis of Rome's general attempt at suppression and extermination until the time of Trajan in the early part of the second century, Beare declines to accept that Peter wrote this letter.

It is fair to point out, however, that outbreaks of persecution occurred in *some* localities of the empire when no similar oppressions were in effect elsewhere. Dr. Herbert Workman, whose historical works have won for him a considerable renown, has made a special study of the early Church in relation to the persecutions that were inflicted upon it. He shows that what we mean today by religious liberty did not exist in fact in the Roman Empire. What did exist was a posture of religious indifference and disdain, which is very different. Religious freedom, including the freedom to *worship* and to *propagate* one's faith, had neither legal sanction nor philosophical approval. Consequently, Rome's way of handling the differences and rivalries between religions was, to use Workman's words, "all a matter of political expediency". What local governors and administrators did in one part of the empire bore little or no relation to what they might be doing in another part. Christians in one area might be under bitter attack, while unmolested in another region.

It is fair to point out yet another thing: competent historians see evidence soon after the great fire in Rome, in the year A.D. 64, that Christians lost their legal status and began to be treated for what they were as followers of Jesus Christ. Prior to this time Rome looked upon the Christian movement as a sect of Judaism. Judaism had long enjoyed a kind of *de facto* legality in the eyes of Rome.

Then came July 16, A.D. 64. A terrible fire raged through some of the most congested areas of the Imperial City. According to Tacitus, the incredibly daring and cruel Nero had given the order for this conflagration and then, to shield himself, had put the blame for it on the Christians. To use Tacitus' words: *"He falsely diverted the charge on to a set of people to whom the vulgar gave the name Christians, and who were detested for the abominations which they perpetrated. The founder of this group, one Christus, by name, had been executed by Pontius Pilate in the reign of Tiberius."*[1]

Even though there were judges in Rome who were prepared to acquit the Christians of this baseless charge, the lie went forth: Christians are incendiarists, Christians are anarchists, Christians are guilty of *odium generis humani*, "hatred against civilized society". Dr. Herbert Workman agrees that we must wait until later emperors, Domitian, Trajan and others, before we see this policy fixed and made general. But he holds that, beginning with Nero, "the question whether a man was a Christian became the most essential part of the charge against him".[2]

Now, if in reading *I Peter*, especially the passage before us, our minds are furnished with knowledge of this background, and if we believe, as many New Testament scholars do, that the epistle was written in Rome in the latter part of 63 or the early part of 64, we can readily see the immense significance of what the Holy Spirit put in Peter's mind to write: "Beloved, do not be surprised at the fiery ordeal which comes upon you!"

When you are thrown into the crucible, don't let it take you unawares.

You will be hated. You will be lied against. You will be put

[1] Cf. Workman, *Ibid.*, p. 29.   [2] Workman, *Ibid.*, p. 29.

to the sword. You will be fed to the lions. You will be fuel for the flames. You will be cast into dungeons. You will be sentenced to exile. You will be torn on the rack.

After pointing out that his language must be understood as that of a "broad survey", and that qualifications and variations must here and there be assumed, Dr. Workman closes his chapter on "Caesar or Christ" by saying:

"*For two hundred years (from Nero on) the leaders among the Christians were branded as 'anarchists' and 'atheists' and hated accordingly. For two hundred years . . . to become a Christian meant the great renunciation, the joining of a despised and persecuted sect, the swimming against the tide of popular prejudice, the coming under the ban of the Empire, the possibility at any moment of imprisonment and death under its most fearful forms. For two hundred years he that would follow Christ must count the cost, and be prepared to pay the same with his liberty and life. For two hundred years the mere profession of Christianity was itself a crime.* CHRISTIANUS SUM *was almost the one plea for which there was no forgiveness, in itself all that was necessary on the back of the condemned as a 'title'. For the Name itself, in periods of stress not a few, meant the rack, the blazing shirt of pitch, the lion, the panther, or in the case of maidens an infamy worse than death.*"[1]

Was this not enough to fill the stoutest heart with consternation?

Does it not fill ours—just to contemplate it?

Yet Peter, by the Holy Ghost, says, "Do not be surprised" at it!

Bring the matter down to our own day. Let the note of warning strike on our own ear. *How little it takes, comparatively, to upset us!*

A Christian man in California loses a valuable orange crop in an overnight freeze and, because an ungodly grower in his

[1] Workman, *Ibid.*, p. 51.

vicinity suffers almost no loss (owing to a slight difference in elevation), comes to his pastor with the querulous challenge, "Why should this happen to me?"

The peril of consternation!

A father, whose boy has lost his life in a motor car accident, puts it bitterly to his minister, "Where was God when my son was killed?"

The peril of consternation!

A minister in London, the morning after a particularly vicious and destructive bombing by the Germans, meets a fellow minister on the street, and, his patience obviously exhausted, says acidly, "I wish I were Almighty God for about ten minutes!"

The peril of consternation!

You might like to know what the pastor said to the self-pitying orange grower. "My dear brother, Job lost more than you have. He lost everything save one—that unshakable confidence in God which led him to declare, 'He knoweth the way that I take, and when He hath tried me, I shall come forth as gold'" (Job 23: 10).

You might like to know what the minister said to the bereaved and bewildered father. "Where was God when your son was killed? you ask. I assure you He was just where He was when His own Son was killed!"

You might like to know what the less agitated minister said to his more agitated brother amid the rubble of a London street: "My dear brother, if *you* were Almighty God for ten minutes, I shouldn't want to live in your universe for ten seconds!"

Somehow the idea has gone abroad—and it needs to be scotched—that if we serve Christ, then God, by some assured intervention, will protect us from adversity, misfortune, persecution, pain. When trouble comes to people obsessed with this completely unbiblical notion, they tend to feel that God has let them down, that He has somehow contracted out of His bargain with them. Peter's tender, realistic Word of long ago needs to be pressed home to such persons: "Do not be surprised at the fiery ordeal!"

When trouble's heavy fist smashes us full in the face, there are four things we should remember, says our apostle.

1. Remember *the purpose that may be assigned to suffering*: "THE FIERY ORDEAL COMES UPON YOU TO PROVE YOU" (v. 12). To prove you! With this we should associate the words of verse 17: "For the time is come for judgment to begin with the household of God; and if it begins with us, what will be the end of those who do not obey the gospel of God?" In both passages the controlling idea is that of *testing, proving*. "Judgment" in verse 17 is not the judgment of doom, as it will be to those who persist in their ungodliness; it is the judgment of revelation, of chastening, of discipline. "Begin at my sanctuary" (Ezekiel 9: 6), said the Lord God through Ezekiel, in reference to the removal of defilement from Israel.

That is where it must begin today, by the way. "Begin at my sanctuary!" There sin must be judged, confessed, and put away. The testing begins there—and often God uses suffering to bring it to pass. Suffering in itself cleanses no heart, rectifies no wrong, purges no conscience. Only the grace of God can do that. But suffering can be employed as a means for humbling us, rousing us, bringing us to self-examination, as members of the body of Christ. "When we are judged by the Lord," said St. Paul to the Corinthians, "we are chastened so that we may not be condemned along with the world" (I Corinthians 11: 32).

Again and again, in its strange and glorious and sometimes sad history, the visible community of God in this world has been sifted and proved by trouble. Deep believers have been shown up for what they are in God. Shallow professors have been shown up for what they are in unreality and instability.

Not long ago I read the testimony of a Christian man in East Germany. He was able to get word to a friend, to whom he confided that his teenage daughter had been refused permission to attend a certain school because of the open Christian commitment of the family. After citing this and other harassments, he wrote: "In spite of it all, we are better off this way, for we know now who are our real brothers in Christ. *There are fewer of us than formerly, but we are closer together, we know what we believe, and we are ready to suffer for it.*"

The Church of Christ, tested, judged, proved—by suffering!

That is one thing to remember, says Peter. From God's point of view the permitted suffering is never without point or value.

2. In addition to the purpose that may be assigned to it, there is that *participation which is afforded by suffering*: "BUT REJOICE IN SO FAR AS YOU HAVE SHARED CHRIST'S SUFFERING, THAT YOU MAY ALSO REJOICE AND BE GLAD WHEN HIS GLORY IS REVEALED" (v. 13). It is in fact a double sharing, a mutual participation—this experience of oneness with the suffering Saviour. We go with Him into the furnace, and He goes with us through the flame. We share with Him in the reproach of His cause, and He shares with us the reinforcement of His courage.

In this you should "rejoice", says Peter, using a word so strong that Selwyn suggests we should translate it "rejoice with rapture".

Think of Geoffrey Bull, at thirty, held for three years and two months by the Chinese communists—part of the time in solitary confinement, half starved, threatened, badgered, cajoled, subjected to the infernal techniques of brain-washing, desperately holding on to some power of objectivity in his brain by making at one time a special study of the six different types of mosquitoes in his cell! And in the midst of all composing this:

> "*Let not Thy face grow dim, dear God,*
> *Nor sense of Thee depart,*
> *Let not the memory of Thy Word*
> *Burn low within my heart.*
>
> *Let not my spirit, Lord, grow numb,*
> *Through loneliness or fears,*
> *Let not my heart to doubt succumb*
> *And keep my eyes from tears.*

Let not the distance come between
As months and years increase,
Let not the darkness close me in,
Let me not lose Thy peace.

Let not the pressure of the foe
Crush out my love for Thee,
Let not the tiredness and the woe
Eclipse Thy victory.

For Thy joy is my joy
And my hope, Thy day,
And Thy kingdom, Gracious God,
Shall never pass away!"[1]

"For *Thy* joy"—the joy of the suffering Saviour—"is *my* joy!"

That mystic participation must not be forgotten.

3. Another thing to keep in mind, if we are not to be bowled over by suffering, is the *power that accompanies it*: "IF YOU ARE REPROACHED FOR THE NAME OF CHRIST, YOU ARE BLESSED, BECAUSE THE SPIRIT OF GLORY AND OF GOD RESTS UPON YOU" (v. 14). Salute the translators of the *New English Bible*, who by capitalizing the word "Spirit" have shown a finer insight than the producers of the RSV. Phillips capitalizes it, as do Moffatt, Cranfield, Selwyn, and even Beare, who has a curious notion that the author of this epistle (writing under the name of *Peter*) has an exceedingly deficient grasp of the doctrine of the Holy Spirit.

As the Shechinah rested within and upon the tabernacle of long ago, the symbol of God's holy majesty and might in the camp of His people, so the Holy Spirit rests in strange splendour and astonishing power on God's suffering people, whose chief

[1] Geoffrey Bull, "Let Not Thy Face", *When Iron Gates Yield* (Hodder and Stoughton, Limited, London), p. 207.

and crucial offence is that they have taken His Son into their hearts and His name upon their lips.

While most of the ancient manuscripts omit what appears to be the last clause of this verse in the Authorized Version, two of the oldest include in the first part of it the phrase "of power", thus making it read, "The Spirit of glory and of power, even the Spirit of God, rests upon you." Recall St. Paul's testimony to the Corinthians. In circumstances of suffering, though not necessarily of persecution, he heard the Lord's promise, "My grace is sufficient for you." To which his soul leaped up in jubilant response, "I will all the more gladly boast of my weaknesses, that the power of Christ may rest upon me" (I Corinthians 12 : 9). The New Testament knows of only one way for the power of the glorified, risen Saviour to rest upon, and abide within, the Christian, and that is through the presence and ministry of the Holy Spirit.

This power in the experience of the suffering people of God is more than fact : it is *glowing* fact.

It *glowed* in Stephen when they were getting ready to batter the life out of him with their pitiless stones: "And gazing at him, all who sat in the council saw that his face was like the face of an angel" (Acts 6 : 15).

It *glowed* in Thomas Bilney, the English reformer who was burned at the stake in Norwich, because of his insistence, as against the Roman Church, that men are justified by faith and not by works. While the fire was being prepared he knelt in prayer not far from the faggots. Those who looked on him saw him praying "with such earnest elevation of his eyes and hands to heaven, and in so good and quiet behaviour, that he seemed not much to consider the terror of death". When his good friend Warner stepped forward to bid him farewell, he wept and Bilney smiled. Bishop Loane, concluding his account of this martyrdom in *Masters of the English Reformation*, says: "Little Bilney had not escaped from death by fire, but those who had eyes to see may have seen that he was not alone: there was one like unto the Son of Man who stood by him in the heat of dying and went with him through the gate of glory."[1]

It *glowed* in John Wesley. In the midst of one of his open-air sermons two ruffians were on the point of hurling stones at him. At the instant when their arms were to let fly Wesley's face became strangely radiant with the glory of God whom he was proclaiming. The arms were slowly lowered, as one assailant said to the other, "He ain't a man, Billy, he ain't a *man*!" Later, as Wesley passed safely through the mob, he moved close to where these young men were standing. Catching sight of them, he blessed them. As he went on, there was another exchange between them : "He *is* a man, Bill; he's a man like God!"

Ah, yes, there's power, even the glorious power of God's Holy Spirit, that accompanies the suffering Church.

The purpose assigned to suffering, the participation afforded by it, the power that accompanies it—these are salutary things to remember. But there is one more thing.

4. Remember the *poise that is appropriate for Christian suffering* : "THEREFORE LET THOSE WHO SUFFER ACCORDING TO GOD'S WILL DO RIGHT AND ENTRUST THEIR SOULS TO A FAITHFUL CREATOR" (v. 19).

You will have noticed how strongly insistent is our apostle-counsellor that the sufferings about which he is writing are endured for the right, and not for the wrong, reasons. It must be pain provoked by those actions, words and attitudes that are pleasing to God. Only then can the suffering be thought of as coming within the frame of His will.

The "reproach" must be "for the Name of Christ". If you murder or steal or commit other acts of wrongdoing against the state and society, you must not call this persecution. As Bigg says, "the times were wild", and it was not unthinkable for false professions of Christian faith to be made. Witness the case of Simon the Magician in Acts 8, an illustration all the more interesting because Tertullian translated Peter's word "wrongdoer" as "magician".

[1] Marcus L. Loane, *Ibid.*, pp. 40, 41.

Nor is it the will of God for you to suffer as a "mischief-maker", which is another word that has fascinated the commentators. Found nowhere else in Scripture or in classical Greek, it means, literally, *one who looks upon, or into, that which belongs to another*. By most scholars it is taken to mean a meddler, the meddling being either into the affairs of others in an offensive way, or, more generally, into things forbidden.

Yes, even the saints can be shockingly nosey. I have known Christian parents who intruded their own views and consciences into the affairs of their grown and married children; and then, when the son-in-law or daughter-in-law turned cold or critical towards them, they assumed an air of injured innocence. If we go around prying when we ought to be praying, we should not be surprised if we kick up a row.

These exceptions aside, says Peter, I call upon you to take your suffering in stride. Go on doing right. Never be content merely to submit to the inevitable. Wherever possible go straight on with positive, active well-doing, and then, whatever the opposition, whatever the cost, "entrust your souls" to God as to a "faithful Creator".

Be quietly committed, even in death, as your Lord was when he said, "Father, into thy hands I commit my spirit" (Luke 23: 46). When they compelled Daniel Cargill, the Scottish Covenanter, to ascend the gallows for his execution, he said, with his foot on the lowest rung, "Lord knows I go up this ladder with less fear and perturbation than ever I entered a pulpit to preach!"

In ways like this, and a thousand more, the troubled people of God have surmounted the peril of consternation and have taken their suffering without dismay.

C. There is the peril of *covetousness*. The danger to which Peter moves next is one that is more likely to beset leaders than others in the Church: "SO I EXHORT THE ELDERS AMONG YOU, AS A FELLOW ELDER AND A WITNESS OF THE SUFFERINGS OF CHRIST AS WELL AS A PARTAKER IN THE GLORY THAT IS TO BE REVEALED. TEND THE FLOCK OF GOD THAT IS YOUR CHARGE,

NOT BY CONSTRAINT BUT WILLINGLY, NOT FOR SHAMEFUL GAIN BUT EAGERLY, NOT AS DOMINEERING OVER THOSE IN YOUR CHARGE BUT BEING EXAMPLES TO THE FLOCK "(5 : 1–3).

The core of the admonition that is here sounded is the issue of *motivation* in the life of a leader. I deliberately use the word "leader" because, while "presbyter" comes close to the Greek word, and while it (or its equivalent, "elder") has the sound of an official title, it is probably fair to say with Cranfield that we should not take it "in too definite and limited a sense". We may think of these elders as holding the office of pastor (vicar, rector, minister) or as holding responsibilities such as are laid upon lay leaders in many of our communions today.

The New Testament has much to say about "elders". The study of the topic is a rewarding one, but too extensive to be undertaken here. The word indeed has a splendid Old Testament background, and thus would have rich associations in the minds of the Jewish members of the congregations Peter is addressing.

The timeliness of the apostle's warning here may be said to grow out of the seriousness of the situation he has just described : a season of crisis and trial, temptations to disloyalty and backsliding, a sifting of God's people through the sieve of their trials. All this requires that the pastoral care given to the congregations shall be of the highest quality. If there is delinquency at the top, the weakness will run down to the bottom.

To point up this peril and to make his appeal for a behaviour that rises above it, Peter brings three considerations before his readers :

1. There is *a fellowship in service to be affirmed* : "I EXHORT THE ELDERS AMONG YOU, AS A FELLOW ELDER" (v. 1).

"A fellow elder!" *That* from Peter, who once peacocked his way to the self-chosen eminence from which he boasted to the Master that the other apostles might all run away and forsake their Leader, but not he!

"A fellow elder!" Just one of the brothers! And, as such,

carrying out the commission he received from his forgiving, restoring Lord, "When you have turned again, strengthen your brethren" (Luke 22: 32).

Strengthen them, Peter, by telling them just what I am telling you: "Tend the flock of God." That is, have a shepherd's heart and do a shepherd's work. The great Bengel suggests that considerations both of *doctrine* and *discipline* in the congregational life must be held in mind by these responsible leaders.

In any case you cannot shepherd them without love and loving care. You cannot shepherd them without feeding them. You cannot shepherd them without training them. You cannot shepherd them without healing their wounds, watching over their strayings, and guarding against their wolfish enemies. And surely you cannot shepherd them without praying for them.

Bishop Stephen Neil tells of the deep impression made upon him when one day the distinguished Indian bishop, Samuel Azariah, remarked that he found time to pray every day by name for everyone in a position of leadership in his diocese. Bishop Neil reckoned that this could mean nothing less than individual intercession for thirty persons, quite apart from those who would be remembered less often. (Some of us might take note of the fact that his rising time was 4.30 a.m.!) Is there any connection, do you think, between these *pastoral* intercessions and the fact that in the thirty years he held the bishop's office the number of Christians in his diocese trebled and that the Church moved forward steadily "in self-support, in evangelistic zeal, and in capacity for responsible self-government"?[1]

Bishop Azariah thus proved himself a "fellow elder" of his clergy and his lay leaders in the churches under his care.

2. There is *a flaw in service to be avoided*: "NOT BY CONSTRAINT BUT WILLINGLY, NOT FOR SHAMEFUL GAIN BUT EAGERLY, NOT AS DOMINEERING OVER THOSE IN YOUR CHARGE BUT BEING EXAMPLES TO THE FLOCK" (V. 3).

[1] Stephen Neil, *On the Ministry* (SCM Press, London: 1952), pp. 107-8.

As a spiritual leader, do you wish simply to be *dutifully professional*? It will not do, says Peter. The "constraint" of which he speaks must be of this order, for it can hardly be physical coercion. "My brothers," cried Samuel Chadwick to his fellow ministers, "preaching must never be a profession: it must be a passion." If our ambition carries us no higher than "bringing off" a professionally decent job, God forgive us. This is a species of covetousness. It is a form of idolatry.

As a spiritual leader, do you wish to make of your calling something *financially profitable*? It will not do, warns Peter. Oh, yes, there is more than a hint in the New Testament that "elders" in the early Church received an income for their services. It could not have been large, but that is beside the point. Some of us have witnessed the corrupting power of money in the lives of Christian leaders even on the mission field, where national pastors subsist with their families on extremely small living allowances.

Actually, of course, Peter's expression, which is translated "filthy lucre" in the AV, has given rise to the almost universal idea that greed for money is the form of covetousness discountenanced here. The Greek text, however, does more than suggest money. The phrase "shameful gain" might as easily be applied to greed for personal popularity or fame, an equally hazardous temptation that lies in wait for ministers of the Gospel. I know of a waggish son who one day said to his preacher-father, "Dad, has anyone ever told you that you are wonderful?" The father said, "No." "Then," replied the son, "wherever did you get the idea?" It's the sort of deflating query that might well be put to Christian leaders whose egos are swollen with ambition.

It might be added that Christ's treatment for this ministerial ailment is crucifixion! Nothing less!

As a spiritual leader, do you wish to make your calling something *dictatorially pretentious*? God will not have it, says Peter. Where the RSV reads "not as domineering", Professor Barclay translates, "not as if you aimed to be petty tyrants". Dr.

D. T. Niles, distinguished Methodist minister and leader in Ceylon, tells of a day in the childhood of his second son when the boy said to him, "Papa, I want to be a preacher when I grow up." His father asked him why. Standing in the church where Dr. Niles was then pastor, the little fellow pointed up to the pulpit and said, "I want to stand inside that and tell everybody what they must do!"

The lad's misconception is forgivable. It is when the grown man, wearing the title of "servant of the Lord", carries this illusion around with him, that mischief is done.

So, whether it be the coveting of pelf or the coveting of power and popularity, the danger of covetousness is never far removed from the heart of the leader.

The flaw in our service must be avoided. If present, it must be confessed and, in the surgical mercy of God, corrected. What He wants is the shepherd whose threefold qualification is an uncoerced mind, an unmercenary motive, and an unpretentious manner.

3. There is *a fulfilment in service to be anticipated*: "AND WHEN THE CHIEF SHEPHERD IS MANIFESTED YOU WILL OBTAIN THE UNFADING CROWN OF GLORY" (v. 4). From Jesus Himself we learn that as the "Great Shepherd" He has risen from the dead (Hebrews 13: 20). Here we learn that as the "Chief Shepherd" He will come again.

How poignant were this man's memories of the Good Shepherd, suffering and dying for the wandering sheep of the Father's fold who must be brought back at any cost! In an intimate flash-back of his own sad experience he tells us that he was a "witness" to the sufferings of Christ—the word here, to be sure, meaning not so much an *observer* as it does one who *testifies to what he observes*. Did he not add to those sufferings with his own fickleness and fear, his own folly and denial?

But then, remarkably enough, he goes right on to say that he was "A PARTAKER IN THE GLORY THAT IS TO BE REVEALED" (v. 1). How could he be a partaker of something that was still future? The answer, as seen by numerous expositors, is that a

preview of the glory of Christ's Second Advent was given on
the Mount of Transfiguration. On that mount, on that day of
dazzling splendour, Peter stood, wrapt in wonder, lost in
mystery, gazing upon glory such as his eyes had never seen
before, and longing that the vision might never end.

The language of II Peter 1 : 16 is vivid and thrilling: "*We
were eye-witnesses of his majesty*." "Eye-witnesses", mind you.
The Greek word means just that. And because we were given
this foregleam, this shining earnest, of the Day of Splendour
yet to come, "We made known to you the power and coming
of our Lord Jesus Christ."

That, says Peter, will be *His* day of revelation and it will
be *your* day of reward. The "crown of glory", *amarantinos*,
unfading as the traditional beauties of the amaranthine flower,
will be yours.

Reference has been made to the martyrdom of Thomas
Bilney, Fellow of Trinity College, Cambridge, and to the farewell at the stake between him and his close friend Dr. Warner.
"O Master Doctor," said Bilney, with a tender, affectionate
voice as from eternity, "O Master Doctor, feed your flock, feed
your flock; that when the Lord cometh, He may find you so
doing. Farewell, good Master Doctor, and pray for me!"

It was the entreaty of a man who could say with Peter, Let
no low or greedy motives flaw your service to Christ and His
Church, that so you may have your work sealed and crowned on
the day of fulfilment, whose dawn no darkness of suffering can
ever hold back.

D. There is the peril of *conceit*: vv. 5–7.

The warning now to be given, like that to the "elders", in
some degree is restricted in its scope. Not so much the whole
congregation as the younger members of it are in Peter's mind
as he says: "LIKEWISE YOU THAT ARE YOUNGER BE SUBJECT
TO THE ELDERS" (v. 5). His concept of Christian submission
—what many New Testament scholars have called the "subordinationist" principle—governs the whole middle section of
the epistle, as we have seen. He returns to it now as he enjoins

a humble and teachable mind on those younger members of the congregation who are least likely to manifest it.

Does our apostle use "elders" in this verse with the same meaning that it carries in the preceding verse? Some say, yes; others, no. Those who say the meaning is different take the word here in its more natural sense of *older men*. The fractiousness and know-it-all air of youth (Wuest thinks that youth-societies were in Peter's mind) frequently require a curbing such as this. What author is it who said, "When I was fifteen I thought my father was hopelessly stupid; when I reached twenty, I was surprised how much the old man had learned"?

But then, with no delay, Peter widens this thought of humility to embrace the whole congregation: "CLOTHE YOURSELVES, ALL OF YOU, WITH HUMILITY TOWARDS ONE ANOTHER, FOR GOD OPPOSES THE PROUD, BUT GIVES GRACE TO THE HUMBLE" (v. 5).

Two pithy directives may be used to sum up what the apostle says in this brief but highly useful section on humility. The first is: Be humble in your *actions*! The second is: Be humble in your *reactions*!

Consider the first. The word for *clothe* describes a thing that is *knotted* and therefore may be applied to the tying on of a slave's apron. You see what was probably in Peter's mind: that memorable night of the Last Supper when neither he nor any other apostle made a move to bathe one another's feet, so peevish were they over the tiff of self-importance through which they had just passed (*cf.* Luke 22: 24), and the Master had risen, laid aside His robe, donned a servant's apron, and had begun washing the feet of all of them. "Memories that bless and *burn*!" And now the words, as they have done a thousand times before, ring like a distant chime through the apostle's mind: "I have given you this example, that you should do as I have done. Truly, truly, I say to you, a servant is not greater than his master; nor is he who is sent greater than he who sent him" (John 13: 15, 16).

Now, says Peter, to his scattered, troubled brethren, let it be understood, once for all, that the wearing of a slave's apron is to be your lot. The Greek form of the verb is decisive. Act with humility. Be the servant of God, be the servant of one another, that our common Lord has shown us how to be and has given us the grace to be!

Then, to drive home the point, Proverbs 3 : 34 is drawn upon (in a free translation) to emphasize the seriousness of this matter: "God opposes the proud, but gives grace to the humble." The proud man has God for his adversary; the humble man has God for his approver.

Let me recall for you some words that gripped me solemnly, from Dr. D. T. Niles' book on *the Preacher's Calling to be Servant*: "It is not merely to the service of preaching that one is called, but rather to be servant to those to whom one preaches. Indeed, the accent falls not on any particular service that one is able or is enabled to render, but rather on one's own status as a servant. It is damnably easy to serve—there are always those to whom we can dole out service—but it is not easy to be a servant."[1]

Yet the great Tauler of Germany, years after he became a preacher, found the way. It was death—crucifixion!

It is still the way.

"If you do not crucify self," cried William Law, "self will crucify Christ. Not as the high priests did many hundreds of years ago, nailing His outward humanity to an outward cross, but crucifying afresh the Son of God, the Holy Emmanuel, who is the Christ. Every man crucifies Christ as often as he gives way to wrath, pride, envy, jealousy, covetousness, disparagement of others, evil speaking, and kindred sins."[2]

If in our actions we are to avoid the peril of conceit and wear the apron of the servant, this death must be ours!

Consider the second directive here: *Be humble in your*

[1] D. T. Niles, *The Preacher's Calling to be Servant* (Lutterworth Press, London : 1959), p. 52 (Harper & Bros., New York).
[2] Quoted by J. Gregory Mantle, *Beyond Humiliation* (Moody Press, Chicago), p. 51.

reactions. "HUMBLE YOURSELVES THEREFORE UNDER THE MIGHTY HAND OF GOD, THAT IN DUE TIME HE MAY EXALT YOU. CAST ALL YOUR CARES ON HIM, FOR HE CARES FOR YOU" (vv. 6, 7).

I have used the word "reaction" because Peter's verb is in the passive voice, giving us the sense of, *Allow yourselves to be humbled under the mighty hand of God.* God's mighty hand is a well-known metaphor in the Old Testament. The Hebrew phrase, as Beare points out, "Usually conveys the thought of God's power exhibited in action in the experience of men, whether for deliverance or for chastisement."[1]

The effect of what our author is saying seems clear: Dear brothers, I know how easy it is for you to fret and fear over the foes you face in this hostile world. I know how tempted you are, within your own fellowship, to worry about position and recognition and reputation. But all of this is really a snare. The trials you undergo are humiliating, to be sure, but God is surely using them for your good. The rivalries and ambitions that threaten to divide and rend you are not easy to cope with, but let each of you realize that God is above and about and within you, permitting all, ordering all, overcoming all, to His glory. Now rest the matter there!

Young Geoffrey Bull, some time before his arrest and imprisonment, while working among the Tibetans, had been dealt with by the Lord on this point of right reactions to difficult circumstances. He had recalled a saying from one of the old saints: "*Many follow Jesus into the breaking of the bread; but few to the drinking of the cup of His passion.*" Reflecting on the searching suggestiveness of this saying, he had written the lines:

> "*O Lord, I have not learnt to cry,*
> *Perhaps I laugh too oft for true conformity*
> *To Thee and Thy rough Cross, or try*
> *To love Thee without sorrowing—*
> *Talk but touch not, thus they heed not.*

[1] Beare, *Ibid.*, p. 177.

What heart, O Lord, moved through the garden?
I too have slept, but wake me, Lord,
E'en though it be to love with tears."[1]

Humility in our actions is becoming and useful, but let us not forget humility in our *reactions*.

E. There is, finally, the peril of *compromise* vv. 8–11.

The letter is now drawing to a close. The dangers that lie along the path of these grimly circumstanced believers must be recognized, and armed against them they must be. There is at least one more danger that will surely arise: the temptation, as Professor Stibbs points out, to give way, in part or in full, when the Devil would "undermine confidence", "silence confession", get us "to stop believing".

Hence come these final appeals: "BE SOBER, BE WATCHFUL!" (Here the staccato terseness of the Greek crackles like pistol shots.) "YOUR ADVERSARY THE DEVIL PROWLS AROUND LIKE A ROARING LION, SEEKING SOME ONE TO DEVOUR" (v. 8).

If we may think for the moment in military terms, Peter is asking for three things:

1. *Never neglect your reconnaissance.*

"Wake! Be on the alert!" is the excellent, dynamic rendering of the *New English Bible*. A sluggish taking for granted that all is well is completely inappropriate to such a life as Christians are called upon to live.

Again, how personally—and painfully—reminiscent Peter must have been in this moment of writing! His anguished Lord in the Garden had said, "Watch and pray, that ye enter not into temptation" (Mark 14: 37). And Peter had gone off to sleep! The sequel, though fully forgiven, was something he could never remember without wincing.

2. *Never underestimate your enemy.*

"Your adversary." That is exactly what the word Satan means. Two titles are put together in this verse. "Devil" is from the word "diabolos", meaning, literally, *to throw over or*

[1] Bull, *Ibid.*, p. 132.

across, and hence, metaphorically, to *accuse*, or *slander*, to evilly *surmise*. Put together all that Holy Scripture says of Satan, and you are still left with mystery. It is not the clearing away of all mystery from the Satan-concept, but the vigorous, unabashed insistence upon the *reality* of Satan, that one finds in the Bible.

Twentieth-century sophisticates say to us, scornfully, "You believe the Devil is real? Come now, I thought you believed in a God of love who rules the world as His own creation. You must be deranged!"

The scorn is itself a sign. A Satan-sign?

The word "deranged" is not inappropriate, especially on the assumption that the cynic is the one who is in fact deranged. For this is a deranged world. It is a deranged world because it is a bedevilled world. Things are upside-down. Values are inverted. The vices and virtues are transposed. The demonic element, when it isn't malignantly voracious, as under a Hitler at his Nazi worst, is incredibly glamorous and cunning, as in the cinema and the novel of our time.

This is your foe, says Peter. Forever the devourer! Take his measure soberly. You will rue the day you treat him frivolously or carelessly.

3. *Never forget your allies.*

As you resist the Devil—for resist him you must in all the immovable firmness of your faith—you will be encouraged by the remembrance that you are not alone in the fight: "KNOWING THE SAME EXPERIENCE OF SUFFERING IS REQUIRED OF YOUR BROTHERHOOD THROUGHOUT THE WORLD" (v. 9).

Although there are numerous difficulties of syntax in this sentence, it is remarkable how uniformly the contemporary translations bear out the thought of being sustained by the assurance of the love, prayers, and the example of fellow Christians who have their own troubles of one sort or another. Moffat, for example, translates it, "knowing that the same sufferings are imposed on your brethren in all the world". Not identically the same, but substantially so!

Deep within the Auca wilds of Ecuador five young mission-
aries are slain. Five widows left behind. Picture them, as one
of them, Elizabeth Elliott, has enabled us to in *Through Gates of
Splendour*, sitting quietly in the kitchen, fingering the watches
and the wedding rings that had been brought back from the
scene of the massacre—trying to work out in their collective
imagination just how it all happened. Which of the men was
first to be lanced? Which one watched the others fall, and was
last to go? What were their thoughts of loved ones left behind?
Did they suffer long? No resting place of certainty for their
weary brains. Mystery. Yet not wholly. "This much we know,"
says Elizabeth Elliott: "'Whosoever shall lose his life for my
sake and the Gospel's, the same shall save it.'"

Before long the messages began coming to them, by letter
and by cablegram, from all over the world. From a college in
Japan, "We are praying for you"; from a group of Eskimo
children in a Sunday school in Alaska; from a Chinese
church in Houston, Texas; from a missionary on the Nile
River in Africa; from an eighteen-year-old boy in Des
Moines, Iowa, saying, "I'm turning my life over completely
to the Lord. I want to try to take the place of one of the
five."

How right was Peter: Whatever our pain or loneliness, we
must never forget our allies! The "brotherhood" is with you,
he declares, in a lovely term that no one else in the New Testament uses, which in fact he seems to prefer to the word
"church".

The promise that now follows brings the epistle to its formal
ending. It underpins all that has been said in this section of
the letter about the perils of which the people of God must be
aware, notably so in times of trouble. More, it underlies all that
has been said about the suffering of God's people, whether
present or future.

Here it is: "AND AFTER YOU HAVE SUFFERED A LITTLE WHILE,
THE GOD OF ALL GRACE, WHO HAS CALLED YOU TO HIS ETERNAL
GLORY IN CHRIST, WILL HIMSELF RESTORE, ESTABLISH, AND

STRENGTHEN YOU. TO HIM BE THE DOMINION FOR EVER AND
EVER. AMEN" (V. 11).

The RSV and the NEB are agreed in the use of this word
"restore". It is not, for my part, the happiest rendering. The
word means to "make whole", and Phillips so gives it. Moffatt
has chosen to leave it "perfect", as it is in the AV. The Greek
word is used to describe what happened when a torn net is
mended, when warring factions are *harmonized*, when dislocated
bones are properly *set*. In short, it means to make *fit*.

Hold this in mind, please, while first we look over the entire
verse as over some magnificent panorama. The centre-piece
of the picture is a pronoun—that little word "himself".

God Himself is the God of all grace, or "every grace", as it
may be translated, reminding us of the word of John in the
Fourth Gospel concerning the coming of God in Christ: "And
of his fulness have we all received, and grace for grace" (John
1: 16). From the grace of justification to the grace of glorifica-
tion—there *He* is. From the grace that searched for me before
I was old enough to know it to the grace that will sustain
me when my dying lips are too febrile to pronounce it—there
He is.

And this God of grace is the God of Glory too! His is the
majesty, the honour, the holiness, the victory Eternal. And He
has called me to it.

This glorious goal is brighter than a dozen suns but the way
to it has darksome valleys that have to be traversed, and black
clouds that hang above it, and fierce storms that break over it.

Yet all the while His grace is sufficient. All the while His
glory keeps beckoning. All the while, in fact, He keeps saying,
"I am your God. I am grace and I am glory. I am your guide
and I am your goal. I am your hunger and I am your food. I
am your thirst and I am your drink."

Himself!

Even suffering can be made to serve—anything can, and
everything—so long as it evokes the exhaustless sufficiency to
be found in Him.

This I will be to you, He says to His suffering people:
I will be your *fitness*.

Some of you have been my children for a long time, but you are not really fit. You are not really abandoned to my will. You are not really sunk down into me as your all in all. You just are not "whole".

And there He stands, wanting me to see that even suffering is a messenger of His, sent to bring me not to lesser life but to greater.

Madam Guyon came to it this way, you remember. Six years of suffering, of loneliness, wearing the spirit of heaviness rather than garment of praise!

And then, her "deeper life" crisis! That July day in 1680 when, as she puts it, "I was set wholly at liberty ... In Thee, O my God, I found it all, and more than all ... What I had possessed some years before was consolation, peace—the gift of God rather than the Giver; but now I was brought into such harmony with the will of God, whether that was consoling or otherwise, that I might now be said to possess not merely consolation but the God of consolation ... One day of this happiness, which consists in simple rest or harmony with God's will, whatever that will might be, was sufficient to counterbalance years of suffering."[1]

Himself!

But He goes on:

I will be your *firmness*. You need to be "established". Barclay says the Greek word means "as firm and solid as granite".

Once more, Peter's word to others is lit up with his own vivid experience. God had done this stablizing thing for him; He could do it for other shaky souls who needed sure foundations.

Himself!

God speaks again:

I will be your *forcefulness*. The word "strengthen" means to be *filled with strength*. One scholar has suggested that the word

[1] Quoted by Mantle, *Ibid.*, pp. 134, 135.

may carry a shade of meaning which says, in effect, I will be the *fulness of your power for active service.* This emphasis is completely appropriate for Peter. Again and again he has said to these battling believers: Do right, and keep on doing it! Be right, and keep on being it!

The power for *that* is what I will give you!

And so John Drinkwater's prayer will be answered:

> "*Grant us the will to fashion as we feel,*
>   *Give us the strength to labour as we know,*
>   *Grant us the purpose ribbed and edged with steel,*
>   *To strike the blow.*
>   *Knowledge we ask not; knowledge Thou hast lent:*
>   *But Lord, the will, there lies our deepest need;*
>   *Grant us the strength to build above the deep intent*
>   *The deed, the deed.*"

CONCLUSION: 5: 12-14

CONCLUSION : 5: 12–14

Although the "Amen" has been written (v. 11), Peter is not quite done. A few matters must be tidied up.

An Appreciation. "BY SILVANUS, A FAITHFUL BROTHER, AS I REGARD HIM, I HAVE WRITTEN BRIEFLY TO YOU" (v. 12). By numerous scholars this is taken to mean that Silvanus was far more than the bearer of the letter. Indeed it is believed that he was substantially more than a scribe who merely wrote down what Peter dictated. He had a hand in the composition.

It has been all but proven—and certainly generally assumed —that Silvanus is the "Silas" of the book of Acts. He was an extraordinary man. He was a Roman citizen (Acts 16: 37). He was a prophet (Acts 15: 32). He had travelled with St. Paul. He was held in high esteem by the churches where he was known.

Was this the moment, one wonders, when Peter, taking the pen from the skilled hand of his gifted companion, writes down this word of tribute to the man who had entered so compassionately and creatively into the apostle's own concern for the embattled Christians who lived beyond the Adriatic and the Aegean Seas? Silvanus must have been dear to him. He had shared Peter's insights, prayed over his counsels, polished his Greek. What a faithful friend and valued collaborator he had been! It was time to acknowledge the debt he owed him. This he does with warm simplicity.

A Summation. With an amazing economy of words, Peter gathers up what he has said in the Epistle, giving his readers the pith and marrow of it, letting them feel again the vigour and urgency of it: "I HAVE WRITTEN BRIEFLY TO YOU, EXHORTING AND DECLARING THAT THIS IS THE TRUE GRACE OF GOD; STAND FAST IN IT" (v. 12).

In the exercise of his apostolic authority he has set out for them the basic Gospel facts and on that solid foundation has urged them to live and act. His swift review of the letter includes both the indicative ("my testimony that this is the true grace of God", so NEB) and the imperative ("Stand fast in it").

It is the putting together of these two—Christ's indicative and Christ's imperative—that makes of any life a pageant of triumph.

> " ' *Lift up your hearts!' We lift them, Lord, to Thee;*
> *Here at Thy feet none other may we see:*
> *'Lift up your hearts!' E'en so, with one accord,*
> *We lift them up, we lift them to the Lord.*
>
> *Above the level of the former years,*
> *The mire of sin, the slough of guilty fears,*
> *The mist of doubt, the blight of love's decay,*
> *O Lord of Light, lift all our hearts today.*
>
> *Then, as the trumpet-call in after years*
> *'Lift up your hearts!' rings pealing in our ears,*
> *Still shall those hearts respond with full accord,*
> *We lift them up, we lift them to the Lord!*"

"Still shall those hearts *respond* with full accord!" That is what Peter is asking.

"Stand fast in it!" It's there for you to stand in always. You didn't contrive it, this matchless grace of the suffering, winning Saviour. You can't generate it. You can only stand in it—forever undeserving, forever undefeated.

A Felicitation. Greetings come next. "SHE WHO IS AT BABYLON, WHO IS LIKEWISE CHOSEN, SENDS YOU GREETINGS" (v. 13). Was it Peter's wife? There is nothing in the sentence itself to make this impossible, nor is there anything, I judge,

in the circumstances that makes it implausible. Or was this
a cryptic way that Peter had of referring to the Christian
communion in Rome? Was it, as the AV has it, the "Church"?
Since it seems clear that "the elect lady" and the "elect
sister" of II John 1: 13 are metaphors descriptive of the
church, it may be best to hold to the traditional view that
Peter here has the Christian assembly in Rome in mind.

The felicitation, as a matter of fact, is compounded. Another
close friend of Peter's, "Mark, my son", sends his greetings.
Could this be more than a friend? Conceivably it could be
literally Peter's son. Probably it was not. What Timothy was
to the Apostle Paul, Mark was to the Apostle Peter—a "son
in the gospel". If we are to bow to an ancient tradition, for
which there is good reason, we may think of these two as having
worked together on the production of the Second Gospel. They
too stood close to one another, even as Peter and Silvanus
did.

Since greetings are in order, Peter now requests that, upon
receipt of his letter, the Christians who read it, or hear it
read, shall "GREET ONE ANOTHER WITH THE KISS OF LOVE"
(v. 14). According to Tertullian, the sacred kiss was called the
peace. Kept within the ceremonial bonds intended for it, it
had beauty. It was the symbol of the Church as a family. At
the same time it was open to abuse. Tertullian alludes to the
objection by heathen husbands on learning that their Christian
wives were greeted in this way when the members of the
assembly came together. Gradually it fell into disuse, much
sooner, however, in the Western Church than in the Eastern.
It can still be found as a practice in groups here and
there.

What is obviously important is that in the "salaam" by which
Christians greet one another, whether it be with palms pressed
gently together in a nearly vertical position (as in India), or
with a low bow and the palm of the right hand on the forehead
(as in parts of the Middle East), or with a clasping of the right
hands of two meeting persons (as in most of Europe and North

America), there shall be the warmth, the good cheer, and the
solicitude of a genuine Christlike love. Without this, even a
kiss can mask a heart as treacherous as that of Judas.

A Benediction. "PEACE BE TO ALL THAT ARE IN CHRIST" (v.
14).

As Peter began his letter, so he ends—with peace.

In between? Ah, trouble, turmoil, tempest, tension! Yet,
beneath it all, through it all, peace!

There must have been a sound in Peter's soul as he pro-
nounced this blessing of peace. It was the sound of music.
Like golden bells chiming across silver seas came the music
of that sentence Peter had once heard in the solemn quiet of the
supper room in Jerusalem, when the shadow of tomorrow's
Cross lay full-length across the whole scene: "In the world ye
shall have tribulation; but be of good cheer, I have overcome
the world" (John 16: 33, AV).

Let us end with two quotations, the first an echo from the
tortured present, the second a witness from the distant past.

Not long ago, some extra hours on an ocean voyage were
improved by the reading of Alan Paton's gripping account of
the agony in South Africa, called *Cry, the Beloved Country.*
There is a passage in which one of the characters turns to
Kumalo, the Anglican priest with the deep hurt in his heart,
and says, "The world is full of trouble . . . I have never thought
that a Christian would be free of suffering, for our Lord suffered.
And I come to believe that He suffered, not to save us from
suffering, but to teach us how to bear suffering. For we know
there is no life without suffering."[1]

Let us listen now to Tertullian, addressing the martyrs of
the fourth century:

*Let us drop the name of prison, let us call it a place of
retirement. Though the body is shut in, though the flesh is
confined, all things are open to the spirit. In spirit, then, roam*

[1] Alan Paton, *Cry, the Beloved Country* (Charles Scribner's Sons, New York,
1948), p. 193.

abroad, in spirit walk about, not setting before you shady paths or long colonnades, but the way which leads to God. As often as in spirit your footsteps are there, so often will you not be in bonds. The leg does not chain when the mind is in the heavens."[1]

Triumphant in trouble!

[1] Tertullian, *Ad Martyras*, 1.2.